HARRIET JOHNSON is a barrister at Doughty Street Chambers specialising in human rights and criminal law and is a fierce advocate of women's rights. She is a founder member of Women in Criminal Law, Joint Chair of Trustees of the charity Women in Prison and in 2016 she founded #DoughtyStWomen events, an annual series of conferences to consider what more the law can do for women. Harriet has given keynote legal addresses around the world, as well as speaking in the media about law and justice, particularly through the lens of gender.

Praise for *Enough*:

An *Irish Times* Book to Look Out For in 2022
A Waterstones 'Best Books of 2022' in Politics

'*Enough* is an urgent and vital call to arms that compassionately and forensically exposes the many ways in which the way we do criminal justice fails women, and offers practical and clear-sighted solutions on how to inject meaningful change into a legal system built by men, for men. Powerfully argued and compellingly written, this is an outstanding debut from Harriet Johnson. It should be read by everybody involved in criminal justice'

THE SECRET BARRISTER

'Harriet Johnson exposes the truth of how misogyny, corruption, underfunding and outdated systems pollute law and policing in our country. With shocking stories from the courtroom and deep research, this book is a powerful, illuminating, enraging and inspiring read for anyone who wants to fight violence against women'

JESS PHILLIPS MP

'Our legal system is failing women. There is a powerful omertà against insiders saying so but things will only get better if they do. A brave and vital book'

JOLYON MAUGHAM KC,
founder of the Good Law Project

'Comes the hour. Comes the book! Here it is – a brilliant, forensic exposure of why women cannot get justice. Harriet Johnson is a wonderful lawyer who captures with rapier precision the way law sustains patriarchy, fosters misogyny and blocks radical change. Women have definitely had ENOUGH'

BARONESS HELENA KENNEDY KC, author of *Misjustice*

'This book will empower the vulnerable and make the powerful empathetic. It's the clearest, most compelling and urgent argument for change. We have so far to go – this book will help us get there'

DAISY BUCHANAN, author of *Insatiable*

'A devastating analysis of how the criminal justice system is failing women and girls, why we need to talk about it and what needs to change'

JENNIFER ROBINSON, co-author of
How Many More Women

'Urgently important'   ALEXANDRA TOPPING, *Guardian*

'A short, urgent manifesto; a stark review of the statistics, which are often worsening. Those stats are peppered with real cases that Johnson has worked on or known ... She is precise, heartfelt and anti-pompous'   *The Times*

'Compelling and forensically written ... She fills pages with vital facts to arm ourselves with so we can destroy lazy arguments. And then she lists what can and should be done to tackle root problems ... It's brilliant, it's comprehensive, buy it. Give it to your male friends'
Evening Standard

'Johnson's book is fuelled by anger ... Johnson writes scathingly about the way women are treated by police and prosecutors'   *Financial Times*

'There is always room for a book this accessible and coherent ... Johnson draws from law, from extensive experience at trial, and colours the text with specific cases ... The potency of these case studies – which almost feel like sad fables – is that the reader can relate ... This is a book of great lucidity, mercifully devoid of legalese despite being steeped in knowledge and experience of the law'   *Irish Times*

Enough

The Violence Against Women
and How to End It

HARRIET JOHNSON

WILLIAM
COLLINS

William Collins
An imprint of HarperCollins*Publishers*
1 London Bridge Street
London SE1 9GF

WilliamCollinsBooks.com

HarperCollins*Publishers*
Macken House, 39/40 Mayor Street Upper
Dublin 1, D01 C9W8, Ireland

First published in Great Britain in 2022 by William Collins
This William Collins paperback edition published in 2023

1

A catalogue record for this book is
available from the British Library

ISBN 978-0-00-853310-6

Set in Publico Text
Printed and bound in the UK using 100%
renewable electricity at CPI Group (UK) Ltd

MIX
Paper | Supporting
responsible forestry
FSC
www.fsc.org
FSC™ C007454

This book is produced from independently certified FSC™ paper
to ensure responsible forest management.

For more information visit: www.harpercollins.co.uk/green

For Keira

Contents

Introduction

*'Not all men practice violence against women but
all women live with the threat of male violence
every single day. All over the Earth.'*
– Fuad Alakbarov

It is impossible to talk about violence against women in
the UK without mentioning the case of Sarah Everard.
Her disappearance and the revelation of her murder in
March 2021 was a terrifying reminder of the dangers
faced by women going about their ordinary lives on a
daily basis.

When the details around her death emerged, grief
turned to anger.

The revelation that she had been kidnapped, raped
and murdered by a serving police officer.

The fact that he had used his warrant card to get her
into his car.

The fact that he had been previously reported for indecent exposure.

The fact that his colleagues had nicknamed him 'the rapist'.

The fact that he was part of a WhatsApp group that shared racist, misogynistic and homophobic content with other police officers.

The violent arrest of women who turned out in their silent thousands to mourn their lost sister, to share their collective grief, to stand for change.

The revelation that an officer tasked with guarding the site of Sarah's body had shared joking memes with colleagues showing the abduction of a woman by a police officer.

The fact that this officer has kept his job.[1]

The subsequent advice from the police, which placed the responsibility for women's safety squarely with women; which told them not to go out alone.[2]

For those of us working in the field of women's rights, each new revelation was all too familiar. We have seen them before.

We have seen police officers committing violence against the women they are supposed to protect. We have seen them use their authority as police officers to do it. We have seen red flag after red flag ignored until it is too late. We have seen police officers mocking, ignoring and belittling women who they are tasked with supporting. We have seen them use racist, misogynistic and homophobic language when they do so. We have seen officers who are policing protests behave aggressively to women; using close bodily contact to intimidate them; exposing their breasts while restraining them.[3] Nothing about the horrific circumstances around Sarah Everard's death was anything less than familiar.

Sarah Everard was not the first. Before her, there was Bennylyn, and there was Jellica, and there was Katie, and there was Tina, and there was Judith. After her there was Geetika, and there was Imogen, and there was Wenjing, and there was Karen, and there was Stacey. Their deaths should each be a stain on the national conscience.

My work as a barrister began in the criminal courts. I had (and have) no agenda in a criminal trial: my responsibility is solely to make sure that everyone I represent, no matter who they are or what they're accused of, has a fair trial. I learned quickly that it is only in fiction that lawyers are on the 'right' side in every case. But early on, I started to notice the hallmarks of a subtler injustice. The prosecutor who joked to me about the likely sexual preferences of his witness. The judge who locked up my client without warning halfway through her trial and, when I raised her caring responsibilities for her disabled son, blithely told me she had 'better give someone her keys'. The police officers who were called to reports of a domestic argument and arrested my client for being 'hysterical', ignoring her bruises and preferring the account of her 'sensible' partner.

More and more, my work has come to focus on representing women, whether that be defending women charged with serious violence in the criminal courts, or bringing civil cases to try to get justice for women who are failed by the police and other public bodies. I have seen how the law can be used to effect real and meaningful change, and how it can fail those who need it the most. I have seen the justice system work to hold the powerful and violent to account, and I have seen those who work within the justice system critically undermine it.

Historically, the law has been slow to keep up with contemporary attitudes to women's rights. As recently as December 1989, a man was acquitted of rape because of the historic presumption in criminal law that a husband could not be guilty of raping his wife.[4] It was not until 1991 that the House of Lords ruled that marital rape was indeed illegal.[5] Even when the appropriate laws are in place, the enforcement of them can render the laws themselves meaningless: at the time of writing, just 1.6 per cent of reported rapes result in a suspect being prosecuted.[6]

Many women of colour, disabled women, homeless and other marginalised women know all too well that the justice system will not help them. It should not take the violent death of another innocent woman for the broader public to realise how dire the situation is. It should not take personal experience of the justice system to learn that it is failing. A functioning justice system is the safety net of a fair society. As with the NHS, we each hope never to really need it, but we must know that if we ever do, it works.

This book looks at the stark facts about violence against women. It examines what we can learn from the data and where the statistics are letting us down. It discusses the failings within the justice system and how we can, and must, implement meaningful changes to make it work for everyone.

It is an appeal for action.

It is a call to arms.

This book does not:

- **provide legal advice.** The law is a thing of nuance, caveats and distinctions. Where it has been necessary to explain the law, I have done so briefly – if I had done so fully, it would have added several hundred largely irrelevant pages to this book. It goes without saying, I hope, that nothing in this book should be taken as legal advice.

- **use only one type of language.** I have worked with, and continue to work with, many women who have experienced violence and abuse of all kinds. Some prefer to be called victims, in recognition of the violence they have suffered. Some prefer to be called survivors, to acknowledge their own power over their trauma. In recognition of this I have used both words. In a legal context, before an allegation has been formally proven, the person making that allegation is called the complainant; there are occasions when I have used that. It is not intended to suggest doubt about what is being alleged; it is simply a lawyer's need for accuracy.

In some cases names, places and other details have been changed to protect anonymity.

Part One

VIOLENCE AGAINST WOMEN AND GIRLS: THE REALITY

Homicide

She provoked him

The Law

- **Murder:** Where a person of sound mind unlawfully kills another person with the intent to kill them, or to cause them really serious harm.

Relevant law: Contrary to the common law.
Maximum sentence if convicted: Life imprisonment (mandatory for all murder convictions).

- **Manslaughter (diminished responsibility):** Where a person kills another intending to kill them or cause them really serious harm but was suffering from an 'abnormality of mental functioning' at the time of the killing so as to reduce their responsibility for it.[1]

Relevant law: Section 52 of the Coroner's and Justice Act 2009.

Maximum sentence if convicted: Life imprisonment.

What the Statistics Say

- In the UK, 93 per cent of murders are committed by men.[2]
- An average of two women a week are killed by a partner or ex-partner.[3]
- Sixty-two per cent of women killed die at the hands of a partner or ex-partner.[4]
- Between 2009 and 2018, 23 per cent of the women over 60 who were murdered were killed by their own son.[5]
- During the same period, in 79 per cent of cases where a woman was murdered by a man, the ethnicity of the victim was not recorded.[6] Where the ethnicity of the victim was recorded, the language used ranged from the meaningless ('Dark European') to the outdated and offensive ('Oriental').[7]
- Of all female homicide victims, 71 per cent are killed at home.[8]
- In 55 per cent of cases where a woman is murdered by a man, there is evidence of

'overkilling' – the use of excessive, gratuitous violence beyond that which is necessary to cause death.[9]

The Fuller Picture

On New Year's Eve 2017, just before midnight, David Clark dialled 999 and told the operator he had killed his wife, Melanie. They had argued. She had told him that she wanted him to leave and that she would call the police to remove him from the property the next day. He stabbed her to death.

At his trial, Clark – a former military medic – claimed that he had suffered a loss of control and so was guilty only of manslaughter, not murder. He claimed this loss of control had arisen after Melanie had taunted him about the size of his penis and as a result of a lesbian affair that he alleged she'd had. Melanie, of course, could not respond to these allegations.[10]

During the trial, newspaper headlines read:

'Murder suspect accused of stabbing wife to death because she belittled the size of his penis claims "lesbian affair" at centre of argument' – *Daily Record*[11]

'Husband killed wife after she mocked the size of his penis' – *Metro*[12]

'Man murdered wife after sending messages to relatives alleging lesbian affair, court hears' – *Independent*[13]

'Estate agent "stabbed wife to death in rage" after row about her lesbian affair and taunts over his "small d**k"' – *Mirror*[14]

'First picture of "lover in lesbian tryst row" which saw estate agent kill wife over "small penis" jibes' – *Birmingham Mail*[15]

'Pictured: the daughter of estate agent's best friend whose tryst with his wife led to murder after she taunted him about his failings as a man' – *Daily Mail*[16]

Each headline, even those published after his conviction, focused on David Clark's story – a story that was rejected by the jury when they convicted him of murder. His false allegations were, seemingly, more interesting than Melanie's silence.

Melanie Clark was the last of the 139 women known to have been killed by men in 2017.[17] Rarely do statistics tell us the full story where violence against women is concerned. When they are full and accurate, they still cannot convey the enormity of its human impact. When they are not, they cannot even give us insight into scope and scale.

When I reviewed the data for this book, marginalised women were frequently made present only by their absence. It is recognised that women of colour, women from poorer backgrounds, disabled women, trans women, lesbians and other marginalised women are more likely to suffer prejudice, discrimination and disadvantage than other women. Yet while these characteristics do not exist in the world independently of each other, statistics that allow us to investigate their intersection are disarmingly rare.

By way of example, while the Office for National Statistics provides an analysis of homicide offences by 'ethnic appearance', those statistics are not currently further broken down by gender, making it impossible to establish whether women of one ethnic group are more or less likely to be murdered than another. The Femicide Census, which catalogues women killed by men in the UK, notes that 'the lack of meaningful, verified data on ethnicity is an ongoing problem' in its research, which results in the census having to draw its data chiefly from Freedom of Information requests.[18] The Femicide Census observes that as well as hindering proper research into (among other things) risk factors, barriers to support and the need for specialist services for women of colour, '[t]he failure to record and publicise demographic data can also feed stereotypes, prejudice and assumptions. Media tends to over focus on the details of violence against women in certain communities and this in turn both feeds and reflects the existing prejudices and racism across UK society.'[19]

While the absence of data means we cannot say definitively whether marginalised women have it better or worse, experience tells us it is unlikely to be the former. When it comes to something as fundamental as the routine deaths of women at the hands of men, lack of information leaves us powerless. We cannot hope to address what we cannot see.

Sexual Violence

What were you wearing?

The Law

- **Rape:** In law, rape occurs when a person (A) intentionally penetrates the vagina, anus or mouth of another person (B) with his penis; B does not consent; and A does not have a reasonable belief that B consents.

Rape, therefore, requires the use of a penis. It is as such extremely uncommon for a cis-gendered woman to commit rape in law, and when she does it is usually under joint enterprise laws.[1]

Relevant law: Section 1 of the Sexual Offences Act 2003.
Maximum sentence if convicted: Life imprisonment.

- **Assault by penetration:** Where a person penetrates the vagina, anus or mouth of another person in the circumstances set out above but using something other than a penis.

Relevant law: Section 2 of the Sexual Offences Act 2003. **Maximum sentence if convicted:** Life imprisonment.

- **Sexual Assault:** A person commits a sexual assault if:
  > they intentionally touch another person;
  > the touching is sexual;
  > the person being touched does not consent; and
  > the person touching them does not reasonably believe that they consent.

Relevant law: Section 3 of the Sexual Offences Act 2003. **Maximum sentence if convicted:** Ten years' imprisonment.

What the Statistics Say

- In England and Wales, 20 per cent of women have experienced some form of sexual assault since the age of 16 (compared with 4 per cent of men).[2]

- Women with a disability are almost twice as likely to experience sexual assault as those without a disability. There is no difference in the figures for men.[3]
- Thirty per cent of female rough sleepers have experienced sexual violence.[4]
- Just 16 per cent of female victims of rape or assault by penetration reported it to the police. Of the women who did not, 39 per cent thought the police could not help them, 25 per cent thought the police would not believe them and 20 per cent did not want to go to court.[5]
- Of the rapes that were reported, just 1.3 per cent resulted in a suspect being charged with a criminal offence.[6] Around a third of alleged rapes that reached court ended in an acquittal or the charges being discontinued, leaving the overall rate for convictions of reported rapes at just under 1 per cent.[7]
- The rate of prosecution for rape has been worsening since 2009 and is now at a record low.[8]
- The low rate of prosecution in rape cases is not, as has occasionally been claimed, because police forces are overrun with false allegations.[9] Research from the Home Office has demonstrated that, at most, up to 3 per cent of rape allegations might be false.[10]

- In the year ending March 2020, 86 per cent of the women who had experienced rape or assault by penetration knew the perpetrator.[11]
- Sixty-four per cent of rapes occurred either in the victim's home or in the home of the rapist.[12]
- In 99 per cent of cases where a woman was raped or subjected to assault by penetration, the perpetrator was a man.[13]
- When women with anxiety, depression or other mental health concerns reported rape, police expressed doubts about the credibility of the victim in 37 per cent of cases, compared with 17 per cent of cases for those without.[14]
- In a 2018 survey 29 per cent of men and 19 per cent of women thought it was not rape when a man had sex with his long-term partner after she had said she did not want to.[15]
- In the same survey, 33 per cent of men and 21 per cent of women thought it was not rape when a woman had flirted on a date.[16]
- In 2019, a survey found that 55 per cent of men and 41 per cent of women thought a woman was more likely to be sexually assaulted if she wore revealing clothing.[17]
- A 2018 report found that 7 per cent of LGBTQ+ people had been offered conversion therapy, which included so-called 'corrective rape' for

lesbian women, in which a woman is raped to 'cure' her of lesbianism.[18]

The Fuller Picture

The statistics show us that the common fear of a stranger raping a scantily clad woman in a dark alleyway is far less likely to occur than an attack by a boyfriend, an ex-husband, a friend, a colleague or a neighbour. So why does the dark-alley myth persist?

Victims of rape have lifetime anonymity, which means not only that they cannot be named publicly, but also that no information can be reported that might lead to their identification. Since most rapists are known to their victims, it is difficult for cases to be reported without giving an inadvertent identification: details of a case wherein the named accused is said to have raped his wife will, inevitably, risk identifying the victim. So we are far more likely to read about attacks on strangers than attacks on girlfriends, despite the latter being far more common.

It is also more comforting to all of us to imagine that the person who might inflict such unimaginable harm would be a shadowy, faceless stranger. The prospect that such a violation could come from a person we know – a person we like, a person we see every day, a person we trust, even a person we love – is unthinkable. Press reports on rapists and paedophiles often resort to using terms such as 'monsters' for precisely that reason. The alternative – facing the reality that most rapists are real-life human beings who walk among us in society; who have jobs, families, children, friends, and yet are still capable of committing this most horrific of acts – is far, far more uncomfortable.

But in denying that reality, and in settling instead for the reassuring myth that all rapists are monsters lurking in the shadows, we harm the women who suffer these attacks. The reason victim-blaming is so prevalent in society is not just because of the ingrained misogyny that dictates everything from how a woman should dress to how she should behave to how clean her house should be and how she should express herself; it is also because we tell ourselves that if the person who was raped did something wrong, then as long as I don't do that same thing wrong it can't happen to me. As long as I don't wear a short skirt, I'm safe. The truth – that you can be in a loving relationship with a person you trust, who makes you feel like the most wonderful person on earth, and that relationship can still slowly dissolve into one of abuse, assault and even rape – is too terrible to bear.

The options for women, therefore, are threefold:

1. **We continue to victim-blame.** We persuade ourselves that as long as we don't behave in the way that *that* woman behaved, we are not at risk. We ignore the realities of the dangers faced by women from every walk of life, in everything they do, every day. We continue to shrink ourselves so that we will be safe.

2. **We recognise the truth.** We acknowledge that the only way to be completely safe is to abstain from:
   > romantic relationships;
   > male friendships;
   > working with men;
   > living near to men;
   > interacting with men in any way.

3. **We force a fundamental change in women's safety.**

Rape myths are deeply unfair, unfounded and damaging to women, but they also do a gross disservice to men. Rape is a crime of violence and power, not of lust.[19] To suggest that a woman was raped because of the revealing clothes she was wearing is to suggest that rape occurs because a man, faced with naked human skin, simply cannot control himself. It is degrading not only to the woman blamed for 'provoking' the attack, but to men everywhere. It suggests that their default position is 'rapist': that the only thing stopping a man from committing rape is a layer of fabric, a lack of opportunity. It is not true.

Sexual offences are perhaps unique in the poisonous nature of their impact. Rarely in life, if ever, do we consent to being hit by a drunk driver, or to having precious sentimental things taken from us in the middle of the night, or to sustaining serious injury at the hands of some stranger. Those things are unequivocally malevolent. But sexual assault takes an act that, when done with consent, can be a joyful and beautiful thing, and is for many people an expression of love, and transforms it into something violent and cruel. The injury of rape is not therefore solely in the harm of the assault itself. It is not just in the humiliation, the shame and the self-recriminations that often follow. It is in the feeling of bitter injustice that comes with being the victim of a crime because of who you are, which makes the attack itself feel somehow more poisonous. It is in the theft of the joy of future intimacy. It is in the knowledge that, if you find in yourself the courage to speak of that most brutal of violations, there will be those who think you are lying. Who would deem it to be in some way your fault. Who would ask what you were wearing.

Domestic Abuse

Why didn't you just leave?

The Law

- **Coercive control:** It is a criminal offence to repeatedly engage in controlling or coercive behaviour towards a partner, ex-partner, co-parent or family member.

Relevant law: Section 76 of the Serious Crime Act 2015. **Maximum sentence if convicted:** Five years' imprisonment and a fine.

- **Domestic abuse:** While there is no specific crime of domestic abuse, any crime that is committed against a partner, ex-partner or family member will result in a more serious sentence for the perpetrator. The judge, district judge or magistrate passing sentence must consider a range of factors including whether the perpetrator took steps to prevent the victim from reporting an incident, whether the victim was forced to leave home, whether the perpetrator has committed domestic violence in the past and the impact on any children.

Relevant guidance: The Sentencing Council's *Overarching Principles: Domestic Abuse* guidelines.

What the Statistics Say

- In the year ending March 2020, an estimated 1.6 million women in England and Wales experienced domestic abuse.[1] The domestic abuse charity Refuge projects that one in three women will experience domestic abuse in her lifetime.[2]
- In the same year, police recorded a total of 1,288,018 domestic-abuse-related incidents. Of those, 41 per cent were not recorded as a crime.[3]
- Women are not only more likely to suffer domestic abuse than men, but they are also more likely to suffer it repeatedly.[4]

- Women are also more likely to be seriously hurt or killed by domestic abuse than men, accounting for 77 per cent of domestic homicides in the year ending March 2020.[5]
- A third of women who die by suicide in England and Wales have suffered domestic abuse.[6] In 2018, 24 per cent of women referred to the domestic abuse charity Refuge had felt suicidal, while 18 per cent had actively made plans to end their lives.[7]
- Black women who experience domestic abuse are 3 per cent more likely to report abuse to police than their white peers, but they are 14 per cent less likely to receive a police referral to Refuge for support than white women.[8]
- Services aimed specifically at supporting women of colour survive on roughly 20 per cent of the incomes of those without such a focus and are more likely to close. There are now only 18 specialist women's refuges run 'by and for' women of colour in the UK.[9]
- Disabled women are more than twice as likely as those without disabilities to suffer domestic abuse. The abuse is likely to be more severe and more frequent than that experienced by women without disabilities.[10]
- Trans women are more than twice as likely as cis women to experience domestic abuse.[11] The abuse

is often focused specifically on the fact that the woman is trans.[12] A study from 2010 found that one in four trans women who survived domestic abuse told nobody what they had suffered.[13]

- A study of homeless women in 2018 found that experience of previous domestic violence was 'near-universal' for homeless women. As a result, many women avoided seeking help from homelessness services that were mixed gender.[14]
- Across the UK, domestic abuse increased during the Covid-19 pandemic.[15] Domestic abuse also routinely increases over Christmas and immediately following football matches.[16,17]
- Pregnancy is an identified risk factor for the beginning or escalation of domestic abuse.[18]
- According to the Femicide Census 2020, 43 per cent of women killed by a male partner or former partner have either separated from them or taken steps to do so.[19]

The Fuller Picture

In January 2014, Valerie Forde texted her sister telling her she was worried about her partner, Roland McKoy. She said, 'Just looking at his face and body language I have to be very, very careful and pray for my safety each day and night.'

By February 2014, McKoy had threatened to burn down the house that he shared with Valerie and their one-year-old, Jahzara, with everyone inside. Valerie reported the threat to the police, who recorded it as a threat to damage property.

Valerie had told McKoy that he had to move out and had set a deadline of 31 March 2014 for him to do so. When 31 March came, McKoy murdered Valerie and Jahzara.

According to the charity Sistah Space, which provides support to women of African and Caribbean heritage experiencing domestic abuse, Valerie's story is not unusual. Ngozi Fulani, the founder of Sistah Space, reports a common theme among the women she helps: 'We are not given the same response [by police] as our white and Asian counterparts ... we're asked, "Where are your red marks?" But some of us have very dark skin. We don't go red.'

The lack of understanding from the police extends beyond skin tone and into culture. Fulani says that the lack of police training can be problematic for things as simple as understanding the meaning of certain language. 'It can be a word like "watch". Depending on the tone and animation you use, it can be a death threat – but that's one small example. There are loads.' She added: 'Without this essential knowledge and training it is practically impossible to cater for, or risk-assess, black women, which puts them at even greater risk.'[20]

Fulani also speaks powerfully about the compound oppression arising from the combination of racism and sexism that makes reporting domestic abuse to the police even harder for black women. 'With the new Windrush scandal, our clients who weren't reporting before are even more mindful. Those who perhaps might report will not now. Even though they have British citizenship, you can't be certain you will not be deported.'[21]

The fear of what might happen after making a report to the police is just one barrier for women suffering domestic abuse. Many of the other barriers are internal. As the domestic abuse charity Refuge describes it:

> An abused woman lives in fear, unable to predict when the next attack will come. She may become isolated from friends and family, and increasingly dependent on her abuser. In these circumstances it can be very hard to make sense of what is really happening. Over time her self-esteem may be worn down, like water dripping on a stone. She may start to believe her abuser's insults. She may blame herself for the abuse, or deny that it is taking place. She may ignore it, hoping that her partner – the man she loves – will change.[22]

The answer to the question 'Why didn't you leave?' is often longer, more complex and considerably more traumatic than the asker can possibly imagine. If we persist in putting the onus on women to solve their own domestic abuse, then, according to the data, our advice must be:

- don't be female
- don't stay – he might kill you
- don't leave, or tell him to leave – he might kill you
- don't be trans, black or disabled (or, if you are, don't expect help)
- don't be pregnant
- don't exist during a pandemic
- don't exist after a football game
- don't exist at Christmas.

The injury of domestic abuse persists long past the relationship itself. The lack of self-worth, the helplessness, the guilt – and, beneath it all, the fear that secretly, in some way, you did actually deserve it. The poisonous legacy of being told repeatedly and consistently that you are nothing, by the person whose opinion you have come to value above all others, lives long.

It also makes each new relationship harder. The dozens of perfectly normal discussions or compromises a person might make during a healthy relationship –

from big decisions, such as your shared approach to money, to tiny ones, such as what film to watch that night – are a hundred times more difficult for survivors of domestic abuse. To be assertive feels dangerous, because in the past it has led to abuse: the ever-looming threat of being left, being hated, being hurt. But to go along with whatever the other person wants feels like a pathway to more abuse; to having less of your self.

Female Genital Mutilation

Not our problem

The Law

- **Female genital mutilation:** It is illegal to mutilate any part of a girl's labia majora, labia minora or clitoris. It is also illegal to assist a girl to mutilate her own genitals, or to aid or abet such mutilation of a UK national or resident overseas.

Relevant law: Sections 1 to 3A of the Female Genital Mutilation Act 2003.
Maximum sentence if convicted: Fourteen years' imprisonment and a fine.

- **Failing to protect a girl from the risk of FGM:** It is a crime for a person who is responsible for a girl subjected to FGM to fail to protect her from it.

Relevant law: Section 3A of the Female Genital Mutilation Act 2003.
Maximum sentence if convicted: Seven years' imprisonment and a fine.

- **Female genital mutilation protection orders:** An FGM protection order is an order made by a court to protect a victim or potential victim from FGM. Examples include an order to surrender a passport to prevent a potential victim from being taken abroad to undergo FGM. Anyone can apply for an FGM protection order with permission of the court. The applicant does not have to pay a fee or reveal their name.

Relevant law: Section 5A of the Female Genital Mutilation Act 2003.

What the Statistics Say

- According to a 2015 report, an estimated 137,000 women living in England and Wales have suffered female genital mutilation ('FGM').[1]
- In the UK, girls most at risk of FGM are often from the Kenyan, Somali, Sudanese, Sierra Leonean, Egyptian, Nigerian and Eritrean communities. Non-African communities that practise FGM include the Afghani, Kurdish, Indonesian, Pakistani and Yemeni communities.[2]
- The 2015 study noted that, while the highest prevalence of FGM is in London, it also affects women in rural areas. The study found that it was likely that every area in England or Wales had at least one woman living there who had suffered FGM.[3]

The Fuller Picture

The nature of FGM makes it extremely difficult to detect. In an attempt to address this, in 2015 a mandatory reporting duty was introduced, requiring health and social care professionals and teachers in England and Wales to report known cases of FGM in under-18-year-olds to the police. However, Dr Sharon Raymond, a GP and safe-guarding expert who trains healthcare professionals in dealing with FGM victims, has described a 'shocking lack of awareness' about what FGM is. She said, 'There is a black hole of data making it hard to analyse the current picture, but from what we know about mandatory reporting, the figures appear very low when we consider the available statistics on the prevalence of FGM in the UK.'[4]

FGM is usually carried out between infancy and the age of 15, before puberty starts.[5] There are four different types of FGM commonly carried out:

Type 1: clitoridectomy: The removal of part or all of the clitoris.

Type 2: excision: Removing part or all of the clitoris and the inner labia, and sometimes also the labia majora.

Type 3: infibulation: Narrowing the vaginal opening by cutting and repositioning the labia to form a seal.

Type 4: All other procedures to the genitalia of women for non-medical purposes, including pricking, piercing, incising, scraping and burning.[6]

FGM is often performed by those with no medical training, using knives, scissors, scalpels, razor blades or pieces of glass. Anaesthetics and antiseptics are not commonly used.[7] Those who suffer it experience physical symptoms, including constant pain, repeated infections, infertility, bleeding, cysts and abscesses, problems urinating and potentially life-threatening complications during labour and childbirth.

Hibo Wardere, an anti-FGM campaigner who was subjected to it when she was just 6, said: 'You can't even breathe and then before you even start to think "What's happening?" it's more cutting and more cutting and more cutting. By the end of it, you just want to die.'

She added: 'I was the person that was being butchered, a child that was being butchered, and a child who saw everything: flesh on the floor, her blood everywhere.'

For Wardere, FGM also had a significant psychological impact. She said:

When the cutting happened, it just spiralled me to a different world where there's a lot of people around you that love you, taking care of you, but you can't see them because you see pain. Then you can't trust them, the trust is so damaged. Even when they call your name, you feel like something bad is going to happen to you.[8]

There is some evidence of specialist 'cutters' being flown into the UK to carry out FGM.[9] However, girls from the UK who are at risk are most likely to be subjected to FGM by being taken abroad to their family's country of origin during the school holidays.[10] To counter this, the government launched 'Operation Limelight' in 2014 to question families flying into and out of Britain at those times when FGM was found to be most likely.[11] The operation has been generally well received, but it has arguably also created racial tensions between the UK authorities and the communities where girls are most at risk of FGM, being branded 'racist' by some of those who were targeted.[12]

In terms of providing treatment and help for those who have suffered FGM, there are just eight specialist FGM support clinics in England, five of which are in London.[13] Despite FGM being illegal since 1985, the first criminal conviction was not until 2019.[14] At the time of writing, it remains the only one.

Stalking

You should be flattered

The Law

- **Stalking:** It is a crime for a person to pursue a course of conduct which amounts to stalking when that person knows or ought to know that their conduct amounts to stalking.
- **Stalking Protection Orders:** a non-criminal order the aim of which is to protect victims. In order for an SPO to be imposed, a court must be convinced on the balance of probabilities (i.e., more likely than not) that: a defendant has carried out acts associated with stalking, the defendant poses a risk associated with stalking to another person, and the proposed order is necessary to protect another person from such a risk.

It is possible for a court to give an SPO without a person having been convicted of a crime. Breach of an SPO is, however, a specific criminal offence, with the maximum sentence being five years in prison and a fine.[1]

Relevant law: Section 2A of the Protection from Harassment Act 1997.
Maximum sentence if convicted: Fifty-one weeks in prison and a fine.

What the Statistics Say

- The number of stalking cases prosecuted has fallen consistently since 2014. Of stalking cases reported, in the period 2020 to 2022 just 6 per cent resulted in a prosecution.[2]
- There is also evidence to suggest that police forces are applying for SPOs less often, with the number of applications having fallen by 31 per cent in the year 2020 to 2021.[3]
- In the year ending March 2020, one in five women had been the victim of stalking since the age of 16.[4]
- A research report has shown that 76 per cent of women murdered by their ex-partners were stalked by the perpetrator in the period leading up to their deaths.[5]

- Statistics from 2011 showed that 80.4 per cent of stalking victims are women, while 70.5 per cent of stalkers are men.[6]

The Fuller Picture

On 8 February 2016 Shana Grice contacted the police to report her ex-boyfriend, Michael Lane, for stalking. Over the course of the previous year she had found Lane outside her house when she left for work, hiding behind walls and appearing suddenly at her front door as soon as she opened it. She detailed how her tyres had been let down on a number of occasions and that the car belonging to her new boyfriend had been damaged while outside her address. Fearing that she would not be taken seriously by the police if she disclosed that she had been in a relationship with Lane, Shana minimised the nature of their relationship when she reported him.

When Lane was later interviewed, he told the police about his previous relationship with Shana. The investigating officer recommended that no further action be taken against Lane. Shana was issued with a fixed penalty notice for wasting police time.

In July 2016 Lane used a stolen key to gain access to Shana's home and watched her in bed while she hid under the duvet, pretending to be asleep. Shana informed the police, who gave Lane a warning not to contact Shana, and a formal caution – for the theft of a key. In the days that followed Shana contacted the police three more times, telling them about receiving persistent phone calls, and that Lane had followed her to work. The case was marked as 'low risk' by the police.

On 25 August 2016 Shana did not turn up for work. A bloody footprint was seen outside the door to her house. Police attended and found Shana dead in her bedroom. Lane was later convicted of her murder.[7]

As for marginalised women, once again the data is missing. Individual stories, however, reveal black women being told they should be 'flattered' by the attention (in one case, after enduring stalking for six years), and that no officer wants to take on their case. As one victim put it, 'When you need help as a black woman no one helps you. I still have fears today.'[8]

Nicola Brookes, a disabled woman who suffers from Crohn's disease, was the victim of a stalker who mocked her disability, made sexually offensive remarks and published her address online. She gave evidence in court that the stalking had aggravated her condition, and observed that 'it should not have taken 3 years and 12 different officers for the case to come to court. I was sending officers around 150 screenshots a day of his persistent behaviour.'[9]

The impact of stalking can lead to significant mental health problems, including depression, anxiety and post-traumatic stress disorder, as well as feelings of fear, distress, anger and distrust, which can remain for many years after the stalking has ceased.[10] Research has also shown that even once stalking has ended, most victims continue to blame themselves for the behaviour of their stalker. In a 2019 survey 83 per cent said they felt they may have done something to trigger the behaviour, and 77 per cent said they felt shame.[11] Stalking victims often experience social isolation, alienation and low self-worth, in part because they reduce their contact with friends and family as a result of the stalking.[12]

Street Harassment

Smile, love, it might never happen

The Law

- **Threatening or abusive words or behaviour:** It is a crime for a person to use threatening or abusive words or behaviour, or disorderly behaviour, within the hearing or sight of a person likely to be harassed, alarmed or distressed by it.

Relevant law: Section 5 of the Public Order Act 1986.
Maximum sentence if convicted: A fine.

- **Harassment:** It is a crime for a person to pursue a course of conduct that amounts to harassment of another, and which that person knows or ought to know amounts to harassment of the other.

43

Relevant law: Section 2 of the Protection from Harassment Act 1997.
Maximum sentence if convicted: Six months' imprisonment and a fine.

- **Exposure:** It is a crime for a person to deliberately expose their genitals, intending that someone will see them and be alarmed or distressed.

Relevant law: Section 66 of the Sexual Offences Act 2003.
Maximum sentence if convicted: Two years' imprisonment.

- **Upskirting:** It is a crime for a person to operate equipment (for example, a camera or mobile phone) beneath the clothing of another person if their intention is to see the genitals, buttocks or underwear of that person, in circumstances where the genitals, buttocks or underwear of that person wouldn't otherwise be visible, and without that person's consent (or a reasonable belief in it).

Relevant law: Section 67A of the Sexual Offences Act 2003.
Maximum sentence if convicted: Two years' imprisonment.

What the Statistics Say

- A 2021 YouGov survey found that 71 per cent of women in the UK have experienced harassment in a public space. For 18–24-year-olds, the figure is 86 per cent.[1]
- The same survey found that 95 per cent of women did not report their harassment (98 per cent for women aged 18-34);[2] 45 per cent of those women said they didn't think reporting it would help.[3]
- According to the Crime Survey for England and Wales, there were around 400,000 female victims of unwanted touching in the year ending March 2018.[4]
- In the same year, there were an estimated 140,000 female victims of indecent exposure.[5]
- Although it now forms part of the Sexual Offences Act 2003 (as amended), upskirting did not become a crime until 2019.
- According to a 2020 report, 85 per cent of trans women have been subjected to street harassment with a transphobic element.[6] Around 14 per cent reported the incident to the police, with those who didn't citing the following reasons:
  - > They felt the police could not help them (70 per cent).

> They expected the police to be transphobic (33 per cent).
> They experienced too many transphobic incidents to be able to report them all (33 per cent).[7]

- A 2018 study by the University of York found that, of the homeless women it spoke to, 'most had been subjected to horrific violations, this included being spat, urinated and vomited on. Many had been robbed, threatened, experienced physical violence and been continually harassed for sex by male members of the public.'[8]

The Fuller Picture

The term 'street harassment' can include, among other things:

- being cat-called/wolf-whistled;
- being stared at;
- inappropriate comments or jokes;
- unwelcome sexual advances or requests for sexual favours;
- being physically followed;
- indecent exposure;
- upskirting;

- unwelcome touching, body rubbing or groping;
- being forced into participating in sexual behaviour.

As for case studies, there are too many for this section. If you are a woman, you already know these stories. You have lived them.

You have been walking in the dark to catch an early-morning train and been propositioned, then followed, by a stranger. You have sprinted away from him towards the lights and CCTV of the train station. You have arrived sweating and shaky, and spent your train journey not sleeping, as others might, but in a corner seat, looking up each time the carriage door opens.

You have been dancing with your friends only to be forcibly grabbed by a drunk man who called you a stuck-up bitch when you removed his hands. Your friends have manoeuvred you to the other side of your circle, away from him. You have spent the rest of your night discreetly looking over your shoulder, always aware of where he is.

You have been on a crowded tube train, becoming more and more certain that the man pressing his crotch against you is doing it on purpose, and not knowing whether to say anything for fear you'll be accused of overreacting. You have looked around, hoping to catch the eye of a fellow passenger who might see what is happening. You have got off two stops early and waited for the next train.

You have gone for a run only to have a man step into your path, grab you, pull out your headphones and demand your attention. You have spent the rest of your run unable to smile at friendly fellow-runners. You have changed your route the next day.

You have been wolf-whistled at by a man in a car while you were wearing your school uniform. You have been told that this is a compliment. That you are growing into a pretty young woman.

You have been sitting on a bus trying to figure out how long the man opposite you has been staring at you; trying to calculate how late you can leave it before getting up for your stop, so he doesn't have a chance to come after you.

You have said, 'I'm really sorry, I've got a boyfriend' – even if you haven't, even if you don't date men, even if you wouldn't touch your propositioner if the survival of the species depended on it – because you know that saying, 'Thanks, but I'm not interested,' can flip a come-on into an assault in seconds. The suggestion that you are already the property of another man is the only way to get out of the conversation safely.

If you are not a woman, speak to your friends. I would go so far as to say that some form of harassment has happened to every woman you know.

For able-bodied, cis-gendered, heterosexual, middle-class white women, the above examples are commonplace. For women who don't fit into that particularly privileged category (as perverse as it sounds to describe a status that leads to such experiences as privilege), the story is more complex, more alienating and significantly more difficult.

For disabled women, street harassment routinely involves strangers exploiting the perceived vulnerability of their targets. Cassie Lovelock, a 26-year-old PhD student, was threatened with rape by two drunk men who pushed her wheelchair along a London street while onlookers did nothing. When she reported the incident to the police she was told 'there's not much we can do'.[9]

The activist Dr Amy Kavanagh, who is registered as blind, has spoken powerfully in the press about her experiences of men grabbing her under the guise of providing (unasked-for) assistance. Men, she states, will often use their pretence of helping her to touch her breasts, make comments or ask inappropriate questions about her body, sexuality or appearance.[10] When Dr Hannah Mason-Bish, an expert in hate crime and gender violence at the University of Sussex, read Kavanagh's accounts online, she looked for academic research into street harassment of disabled women. She found none.[11]

She and Kavanagh have since founded the 'Private Places, Public Spaces' blog, where disabled women and non-binary people share their experiences of non-consensual touching. Its posts are compelling and illuminating and alarming reading.[12]

For women of colour, 'standard' street harassment often includes racist overtones, which become more explicit when the woman being harassed has made it clear that the advances are not welcome. In '*I'd Just Like to Be Free*', a short film made by black feminist organisation Imkaan and the End Violence Against Women Coalition, young women described their experiences:

> After me ignoring them, that's when it turns racial – that's when it might be 'you black this' or 'you black that, how dare you ignore me'.

> ... being called a black whore because you wouldn't give your number away to some guy in a club ...

> The next thing you know he starts making monkey noises at me, and I'm just like, okay, so you go from objectifying me, from me being, like, this sexual thing to you, and then when you get rejected you think it's okay for you to then shout racist taunts.[13]

In written evidence presented to the Home Affairs Committee inquiry into violence against women and girls, the campaign group Our Streets Now relayed these accounts:

We were walking back from the pub with our other friends and walked past some guys who said really loudly as they walked past me and my partner, 'What a fucking waste, I'd love to smash her,' referring to me, maybe because I don't look stereotypically 'gay'.

You also get men who harass you and then take your rejection as an excuse to express their racism. You go from being 'sexy legs' to a 'dirty P*ki' in a matter of minutes.

I get a man on a train telling me, 'Ooh, love, did someone fuck you too hard and now you're broken?' [...] This needs to be illegal. This needs to stop. For me, I thought becoming disabled would be my hardest battle, but now the anxiety of going out, feeling at my weakest and facing harassment on a daily basis, has become my normal.

One day on my way home from school, in my school uniform, a group of men started sexually harassing me. I turned around and told them I was 13; their response was, 'Age doesn't matter to us.'

Muslim women, especially those who wear the niqab, are met with remarks such as:

'Why do you have a mask on? Are you really ugly under there?'

'I want to cut that black thing off your face.'

'Are you carrying a belt full of explosives?'

'Why are you dressed like that? Are you a suicide bomber?'

One woman described having her niqab forcibly removed:

Taking the veil off is equal to rape, really. I was walking down the street in the local area [in Leicester] and there were three white men in their early twenties. They took my niqab off from behind. I tried to conceal my face with my scarf and then, when I tried to retrieve my niqab, they wanted to take a look at me. They bent down to see what I looked like and then they chucked it on the floor.[14]

Online Harassment

Just don't look at it

The Law

- **Malicious communications:** It is a crime to send to another person an electronic communication that is threatening, indecent or grossly offensive.

Relevant law: Section 1 of the Malicious Communications Act 1988.
Maximum sentence if convicted: Two years' imprisonment and a fine.

- **Improper use of a public electronic communications network:** It is an offence to send a message or other matter that is grossly offensive or of an indecent, obscene or menacing nature.

Relevant law: Section 127 of the Communications Act 2003.

Maximum sentence if convicted: Six months' imprisonment and a fine.

- **Disclosing private sexual photographs and films with intention to cause distress:** It is a crime for a person to disclose a private sexual photograph or film without the consent of the individual appearing in it and with the intention to cause that person distress.

Relevant law: Section 33 of the Criminal Justice and Courts Act 2015.

Maximum sentence if convicted: Two years' imprisonment and a fine.

What the Statistics Say

- According to a 2017 poll by Amnesty International, 20 per cent of women in the UK have suffered online abuse or harassment.[1]
- Nearly half of women who have been abused or harassed online said the content was sexist or misogynistic, while 27 per cent were threatened with sexual or physical assault.[2]

- Of the women who suffered online abuse, 55 per cent experienced anxiety, stress or panic attacks as a result.[3]
- In a 2021 study, 69 per cent of women said the abuse or harassment experienced by MPs would put them off seeking public office.[4]
- Black female journalists and MPs are 84 per cent more likely to receive abusive tweets than white women.[5]
- In the UK, 15 per cent of people between the ages of 18 and 45 have had intimate pictures of them shared without their consent. Women account for more than 75 per cent of victims.[6]
- A 2021 study found that 75.8 per cent of girls between the ages of 12 and 18 had been sent an image of male genitalia.[7]
- In the same study, 41 per cent of girls spoken to reported having been asked to send a sexual image of themselves, compared to 17.5 per cent of boys. Of those who had been asked, girls felt more pressure to do so than boys.[8]
- More than half of the children who had received unwanted sexual content online, or had an image of them shared without consent, did not tell anyone or report the perpetrator.[9]

The Fuller Picture

Phoebe Nelson began posting body-positive content to her Instagram account when she was a teenager. When she posted a photo to mark International Women's Day in March 2020, she was trolled about how she looked. It escalated to the point where she was being abused online every day. She blocked and reported each account responsible, to the point where she had blocked nearly 10,000. She estimates that at the height of the abuse she was receiving around 100 death threats a day. When she reported these death threats to the police, they advised her to log off from social media.

In December 2020, unable to cope with the abuse, she attempted suicide and was hospitalised. When she later posted about her suicide attempt she received more abuse.[10]

Online abuse is especially prolific towards women in public life, and especially towards women of colour. A study by Amnesty International monitored the online abuse received by female MPs in the run-up to the 2017 election. It found that black and Asian women MPs received 35 per cent more abusive tweets than their white counterparts. It affected women of all parties. Diane Abbott, who has been a Labour MP for Hackney North and Stoke Newington since 1987, received almost half of all abusive tweets in the weeks preceding the election.[11]

Speaking in Parliament at a debate about the abuse and intimidation of MPs, Diane Abbott said:

> In my case, the mindless abuse has been characteristically racist and sexist. I have had death threats, and people tweeting that I should be hanged 'if they could find a tree big enough to take the fat bitch's weight'. There was an English Defence League-affiliated Twitter account – #BurnDianeAbbott. I have had rape threats and been described as a 'pathetic useless fat black piece of shit', an 'ugly fat black bitch' and a 'n*gger' – over and over again. One of my members of staff said that the most surprising thing about coming to work for me is how often she has to read the word 'n*gger'. It comes through in emails, Twitter and Facebook.[12]

Research by the Centre for Countering Digital Hate has found that 97 per cent of accounts sending misogynistic abuse on Twitter and Instagram were allowed to remain on the sites after being reported.[13]

The last decade has seen the rise of the so-called 'incel' movement, comprised of men calling themselves 'involuntary celibates' and blaming women for their perceived lack of sexual and social status. Since 2014, men calling themselves incels have carried out mass killings in the US and Canada.[14] In Plymouth in 2021, Jake Davison shot and killed five people, injuring two others, before fatally shooting himself. In the aftermath of the murders, it emerged that Davison had links to the incel movement and had expressed misogynistic and homophobic views online.[15]

Research from *The Times* and the Centre for Countering Digital Hate has shown that in the eight months leading up to November 2021 alone, UK traffic to three of the most prominent incel websites increased more than 550 per cent.[16]

A Culture of Violence and its Impact on Women

What the Statistics Say

- Women who have experienced harassment are more likely to feel unsafe when walking alone, even during the daytime and in busy public spaces.[1]
- In 2021, 50 per cent of women surveyed said they would feel unsafe walking on their own, after dark, in a quiet street near their home. The number for men was 17 per cent.[2]
- Disabled women felt less safe walking alone than non-disabled women.[3]
- According to the same survey, 20 per cent of women had stopped leaving home alone during the daytime as a result of feeling unsafe when doing so (at night, this rose to 24 per cent), while 26 per cent of women had stopped walking in

quiet places or open spaces during the day (which rose to 32 per cent at night).[4]

- According to a 2018 report, 67 per cent of parents have told their daughters not to walk home after a certain time; 47 per cent have told them not to go to certain places; 41 per cent have told them not to go out after dark, and 40 per cent have told them not to take certain routes home.[5]

Many women don't notice the tiny changes we gradually make to our behaviour, because every minute thing we do is, in reality, part of an exercise in self-deception; a lie we tell ourselves about having a modicum of control. We don't notice our world shrinking or the constant, calculated adjustments we make to try to make our everyday lives less dangerous. To make our mere existence less of a threat to our lives.

When Sarah Everard went missing I told my mum, 'Don't worry, I literally never go out anymore.' It was meant as a joke about my own social habits, or lack thereof. But it revealed more than I had meant it to about the way women reassure themselves, and others who care about them.

A woman was taken off the street and murdered. Don't worry, I won't go out.

Most women who are murdered die at home. Don't worry, I won't stay in.

A woman was targeted on a dating app – don't worry, I'll have a friend nearby. I'll call to let you know I'm okay. I just won't date.

A woman was attacked in the street. Don't worry, I'll ignore him. Or I won't, because that might make him angrier. I'll smile and placate him until I'm in a safer space. Or I won't, because that's leading him on. I'll tell him to leave me alone. Or I won't, because that might make him attack me.

The bitter reality is that there is nothing we can do to make ourselves safe. Sarah Everard was walking a short distance home. She was not wearing revealing clothing. She did not flirt with anyone. It was not late at night. The man who stopped her was a police officer. She properly complied when he showed her his warrant card.

No woman can make herself small enough to be safe from this violence.

No woman should have to.

Part Two

A JUSTICE SYSTEM THAT FAILS WOMEN

Fair Trials

The right to a fair trial is a fundamental cornerstone of democracy; it is not hyperbolic to say that without it we dissolve into a police state. Most of us in our lives have been falsely accused of something. Happily, it's not usually a crime – for me, the example that always springs to mind is being accused of 'starting it' when arguing with siblings as a child. I remember so vividly that grasping stomach ache of knowing the truth but not being able to prove it. Of thinking, 'If I could show you inside my head, I could show you that that's not true,' but not being able to do so. It is a horrible feeling.

Needless to say, the consequences of a criminal conviction are far more serious than a telling-off from your mum. A criminal conviction can prevent you from being able to do certain jobs, like teaching or care work. It can be taken into consideration in future court proceedings, like those that determine custody of children following a separation. It can stop you being able to travel to certain countries, including the USA. And, of course, in many cases it carries the very real threat of prison.

Despite what certain newspapers might have you believe, prison is not comfortable. It is not a holiday camp where you are issued with your own Xbox, massage chair and cuddly toy on arrival. In the year ending June 2021, 81 people in prison died by suicide. In the same year, there were 53,290 incidents of self-harm and 19,470 assaults.[1] Many of those sentenced to periods in prison subsequently experience homelessness, unemployment and the break-up of their family.[2]

Which is why, if we are going to convict people of a criminal offence, the least we can do is ensure that a trial is fair. The right of a person – no matter how awful we might consider that person to be, and no matter how heinous the crimes of which they are accused – to be able to see the evidence against them, and to challenge that evidence properly before a jury of their peers, is fundemental. As Sarah Vine KC put it, 'Rights aren't rights unless you extend them to people you loathe – otherwise they're just favours.'

You will not find, in this book, any criticisms of people who uphold the right to a fair trial for those accused of committing violence against women. But it is possible for a justice system to protect women without undermining the rights of the accused. As things stand, ours does not.

From the police, to the Crown Prosecution Service, to the courts themselves, our justice system routinely fails women.

Policing Women

A significant part of my work involves trying to help women who have been subjected to serious violence and have reported it to the police, only to be told that nothing can be done. When a new case comes in, it usually involves a written cover letter from the solicitor who has hired me, giving a summary of the facts of the case. For most of these summaries, the first pages are eerily similar. They start with an account of the attack suffered: the abuse, the domestic violence and, usually, the rape. Halfway down the page, it details how the woman in question went to the police and told them what had happened. By the bottom of the page, she has been told that there is nothing that the police can do. Whether for lack of forensic evidence, or the simple fact that the police do not deem her to be believable, they cannot proceed with a prosecution.

Before I have turned the page, I know that at the top of page two the story will continue in one of two ways: 'And then he did it again.' Or: 'And then he killed her.'

I know these words are coming. That does not stop them thudding through my stomach when they do.

By definition, the cases I see are not the ones where things went well. If a police officer did an excellent job making a rape victim feel comfortable, enabling her to give the best evidence she can about what happened, finding independent evidence to corroborate her allegation and supporting her through the justice system to get a conviction at court, her case is unlikely to land on my desk. I have an inherently skewed data sample. But the stories in the cases I see are too awful, and have too much in common, to allow them to be written off as the one-off failings of an occasional rogue officer in need of more training.

One of my clients, who had been drugged and raped at a party, went to the police to tell them that she thought something had happened the previous night – she couldn't be sure, but she had a strange feeling. She was examined by a specialist forensic unit and the results were awaited. When the forensic report came back, it was read by a junior female officer. She emailed her supervisor, who had also worked on the case, telling him: 'Surprise, surprise, forensics show nothing.'

He replied: 'You're kidding? But she had a funny feeling and everything!'

But the forensics didn't show nothing. The forensic report, which had been misread by the junior officer, in fact showed the presence of semen: independent evidence that, in conjunction with the woman's account of being drugged, could have supported a prosecution for rape. The report's writer recommended further tests be carried out on the clothing of the suspect – clothing which, by the time the report was read properly, had been returned to him.

In another case, my client reported her rape and gave a detailed video interview of what had happened. She was told that there was not enough evidence to prosecute her rapist. Years later, two weeks before her wedding, a police officer knocked on her door. My client saw the uniform and said, 'He's done it again, hasn't he?'

The officer explained that her rapist had indeed been accused of rape by another woman, and that the police were now hoping to prosecute both cases at once, as they were factually very similar. They hoped this would help them to get a conviction. My client was told she would have to be video-interviewed again. She asked why, since her first account had been video-recorded. She was told that the DVD containing the filmed account of her rape had been lost.

In another case, my client reported that her husband had raped her and attempted to rape another woman who had severe learning disabilities. She gave an account to the police, and also showed them messages in which he had threatened to kill her. She waited and waited to be told what was happening to her case. Over a year later, while still under investigation, her rapist raped, then murdered, another woman.

In another case, the forensic swabs – containing crucial DNA evidence that supported my client's allegation of rape – were lost by police. Her case was abandoned.

In yet another, an officer emailed his colleague telling him an allegation of rape was 'plainly bollocks and would never see a courtroom'.

Disbelief or pre-judgment of victims is part of a culture of victim-blaming and rape denial that pervades in the UK. The police are drawn from society and have the same biases and prejudices as the rest of us – the difference is that they have weapons, they have power and they have authority.

These biases and prejudices are significantly more visible when it comes to marginalised women. DC Maggie Oliver spent months gaining the trust of girls who had been victims of the Rochdale grooming gang. Two of the girls spent six months doing repeated video interviews and ID parades, in which they disclosed rape by over 20 offenders. When the officers running the investigation decided not to use their evidence in the prosecution, DC Oliver protested. She was told, 'Maggie, let's be honest about this. What are these kids ever going to contribute to society? In my opinion, they should have just been drowned at birth.'[1]

Disabled women who have experienced sexual violence have reported being met with prejudice, ableism and a lack of understanding when relaying their allegations to police officers. One, who has autism and PTSD, was told that she was not a reliable witness because her conditions made her 'overly emotional'. Another, who is blind, has reported ten different sexual assaults by strangers on tube carriages and at stations – where CCTV is routinely available. Each time she reports one of these crimes her allegations are dismissed because she 'cannot identify her perpetrators'.[2]

A client of mine was told by officers that her anxiety and depression, which she began to suffer after her rape, meant that she would not be deemed credible by a jury and so they could not prosecute her case. Any decent prosecutor would have drawn an evidential line between the attack and the consequences, making the point that the psychiatric injuries she had suffered were evidence of the attack having happened. The decision of the police not to take any further action meant no lawyer had the chance to look at it.

Pre-judgment of what a jury might think is, in my experience, a central and systemic problem with the police when it comes to prosecuting violence against women. I have had more than one client attend a police station to report serious violence, only to be told that she must hand over her mobile phone as she does so. Without this, women are told, police cannot possibly prosecute. Many are understandably reluctant: most of us rely on our mobile phones for a range of day-to-day practical uses. For people who are processing trauma, it can be more important than ever to be able to be in consistent contact with friends and loved ones. Already nervous and anxious about reliving their experience through the process of going to court, many women choose not to hand over their telephones, inviting the inspection of every tiny detail of their private lives, while simultaneously robbing them of the ability to retain contact with their support networks.

The reality is that the refusal to hand over a mobile phone *can* impact on a prosecution. A defence barrister might, quite properly, make the point to a jury that as the victim has not handed over her phone, there might be evidence relevant to the case that they have not seen. The prosecution barrister might argue that she is entirely within her rights to do so, that perhaps she has been forced to expose enough about the intimate parts of her life. The jury would consider those matters, along with the rest of the evidence it has heard, in reaching its decision. But it would, at least, be a jury decision. The absence of a phone is not in itself a reason to abandon hope of a conviction.

The decision of whether or not to prosecute serious crimes is usually made by the Crown Prosecution Service (CPS), having had a case referred to them by the police.[3] However, many cases are not referred to the CPS for advice as a result of decisions made by police officers. According to a 2018 study, in 29 per cent of sexual assaults reported to the police, the crime report was subsequently cancelled due to the police concluding that 'no crime' had occurred.[4]

The test for whether or not to prosecute has two parts: the evidential test, and the interests of justice test. The evidential test is whether or not, based on the evidence available and bearing in mind any defence that is likely to be raised, there is a realistic prospect of conviction. The test assumes that a jury deciding the case will be impartial and reasonable, and will act in accordance with the law. The interests of justice test is, simply, whether it is in the interests of justice to prosecute the case.

In the most serious cases, it is a jury that determines the result of a trial. For a jury to convict someone of a criminal offence, they must be sure of guilt. No further explanation on what 'sure' means is given to them – it is an ordinary word, and juries are told to give it its ordinary meaning. This has been referred to as the 'acquittal bias' and is based on a historic legal rule known as Blackstone's ratio: namely, the principle that 'it is better that ten guilty persons escape than that one innocent suffer'.[5]

Before a jury goes to consider its decision, having heard all of the evidence, it is given standard directions on the law from the judge in charge of the trial. These instructions include the importance of trying the case on the evidence alone, the fact that in order to convict they must be sure, and directions on how to approach any other aspects of the law that might have come up during the trial. One relatively new instruction is the direction on sexual offences and stereotypes. Juries are told:

> The experience of judges who try sexual offences is that an image of stereotypical behaviour and demeanour by a victim or the perpetrator of a non-consensual offence such as rape held by some members of the public can be misleading and capable of leading to injustice. That experience has been gained by judges, expert in the field, presiding over many such trials during which guilt has been established but in which the behaviour and demeanour of complainants and defendants, both during the incident giving rise to [the] charge and in evidence, has been widely variable. Judges have, as a result of their experience, in recent years adopted the course of cautioning juries against applying stereotypical images of how an alleged victim or an alleged perpetrator of a sexual offence ought to have behaved at the time, or

ought to appear while giving evidence, and to judge the evidence on its intrinsic merits. This is not to invite juries to suspend their own judgment but to approach the evidence without prejudice.[6]

A judge may not use these exact words: they will usually tailor the directions given to a jury according to the facts of the case. But the warning is there; it is one of the last things that a jury hears before it goes to consider its verdicts.

Most barristers will tell you that, out of juries and magistrates, a jury will usually give a fairer verdict – for the simple reason that those who deal with the same sorts of cases on a daily basis can lose perspective and balance. It is hard to continue to evaluate the evidence in your hundredth case with the same vigour as you applied to your first. It is not a deliberate decision to treat one case any less fairly than another – it is an inevitable consequence of hearing something over and over. It is called becoming case-hardened, and it is something from which, in my view, many magistrates can suffer. A jury – even a second-week jury, perhaps hearing its second trial – hears the evidence afresh and (at least in my experience) listens carefully to the directions given by a judge.

Which is why it is so problematic when case-hardened police officers decide that a jury would not believe the word of a rape victim; that a jury would ignore the directions of a judge telling them to leave prejudice at the door; that a jury, made up exclusively of people who watch too much *CSI*, want everything to be tied up with forensics, eyewitnesses, CCTV, a full confession and a nice bow before it would convict; that people are not smart enough to appreciate that real life is not like that.

I have seen successful rape prosecutions with no forensic evidence, no DNA evidence, no CCTV and no eyewitnesses – prosecutions that rely on nothing more or less than the victim's word, and a skilled and fair prosecutor. I have heard closing speeches that make a jury really feel what the victim was feeling in a way that could not be clearer if they could see inside her head for themselves. I have seen jurors reduced to tears listening to the evidence of a woman describing, dry-eyed and stoic, the worst thing that has ever happened to her. Any lawyer who has spent time in a criminal court will be able to tell you the same.

So when police officers decide that a jury would not believe a victim, on the basis of their own prejudicial, bigoted or simply case-hardened ideas about rape, they are undermining the function of a jury and, in turn, the rule of law in this country. When juries are sworn in at the start of any criminal trial, they promise 'to faithfully try the defendant and give a true verdict according to the evidence'. Evaluating the evidence is at the heart of a jury's role. Yet with charging rates for reported rapes at just 1.6 per cent, the consequence is that, in 98.4 per cent of cases, juries do not get that opportunity.[7]

The consequence of poor investigations – where evidence is lost, where reports are misread and where women are disbelieved – is not just that the conviction rate for reported rape languishes at 1 per cent. It is not just the loss of goodwill from the victim, who may not be prepared to help the police the next time they come knocking, asking her to put herself through reporting it again. It is not even just about the compounded harm done to the victim: the cumulative damage of going through one of the worst traumas a person can experience, only to be told by people in uniform, whose job it is to support you, that in their professional opinion you are not worthy of being believed. It is that a person who has committed a serious crime remains at large, free to do it again to some other woman who crosses his path. It is the constant, quiet message that 99 per cent of rapists go free, which tells women that their safety is not a priority, and tells the man already looking for an excuse that a cheeky grope when she's drunk or passed out really isn't that bad.

I have met and worked with many truly excellent police officers. People who joined the police for the very best reasons, and who with utter selflessness put their very lives at risk to protect people they have never met. They do so in exchange for low pay and antisocial hours, and in the knowledge that they are expected to be on duty at a moment's notice. In the year ending March 2021, there were nearly 37,000 assaults on police officers: an average of over a hundred a day.[8] It is a thankless job, and one that I freely admit I would not wish to do.

As well as dealing with the inevitable challenges that come with such a difficult job, these same officers have faced funding cuts of 16 per cent and a drop of 15 per cent in the number of officers since 2009/10, with crime rates continually increasing.[9] A recent investigation by the *Guardian* newspaper found that at least 40 per cent of police forces in England and Wales lack specialist rape units.[10] Responding to the figures, the director of the End Violence Against Women Coalition, Andrea Simon, described the figures as 'highly concerning', observing that 'we have lost vital expertise in investigating and prosecuting sexual violence as a result of several of these units being dissolved due to funding cuts in recent years'.[11]

Cuts to mental health provision and youth services have not only meant that the long-term benefit of those services in supporting people who might otherwise end up committing criminal offences has been lost, but also in the short term that police officers have to step in to deal with more incidents that would be better dealt with by specialist resources, which are now no longer available.[12]

It is not just the lack of officers the police has to battle against. A lack of financial resources sees officers pressured to be selective about which evidential tests to run: if the prospects of a forensic test returning a meaningful result are low, officers are instructed not to expend limited police resources on running it.[13] Key forensic analysis is now routinely outsourced to private companies by police forces, leading to what has been called a 'race to the bottom' where, it is claimed, police contracts for forensic analysis work are awarded to the lowest bidder, regardless of whether those laboratories complied with the minimum standards set by the government. Concerns have been raised about the quality and reliability of the forensic evidence produced as a result.[14]

The increasing speed of developments in technological capability has left police forces up and down the country unable to cope with the impact on criminal investigations. Where previously a mobile phone held limited information on a small amount of memory, now the tiny computers that we carry in our pockets contain more information and capability than the most powerful commercially available desktops had 30 years ago. To obtain, download and process this information takes weeks of police time that is simply not available. Police officers are forced to cut corners, searching for key words or dates rather than reviewing all of the evidence there is, and running the risk of missing crucial details. The specialist training required for all officers, not just for those operating in cybercrime, is complex and needs to be constantly renewed and updated.

Finally, it was announced in April 2021 that the government planned to introduce crime targets for the police in exchange for its promised 20,000 new officers, to add to the existing 135,000 already in service. The Police Federation of England and Wales said the plans would 'result in a return to a damaging, target-driven culture'. Its chair, John Apter, made the point that 'when resources become scarce, forces focus on targets to the exclusion of other issues'.[15] That is something that has been confirmed to clients of mine by the officers who have told them their cases cannot proceed. They are told that high expectations and scarce resources mean they have to focus on only the most 'promising' cases. As if they were backing a racehorse. As if that made it all right that their attacker – indeed, the majority of attackers – were free.

While the focus has long been on the question of whether or not the police can or will properly investigate violence against women, there is a still more serious problem that requires urgent attention: when it is police officers themselves who are the offenders.

In the aftermath of the conviction of PC Wayne Couzens for the rape and murder of Sarah Everard in

March 2021, DCI Simon Harding told reporters that police officers viewed Couzens not as a police officer who was a murderer, but as 'a murderer who happened to be a police officer'. When Couzens first admitted responsibility for Sarah's death Dame Cressida Dick, then Metropolitan Police Commissioner, described the police as a body where you might find 'on occasion ... a bad 'un'.

Yet the details that emerged as the case progressed provided little reassurance: the revelation that other officers had nicknamed Couzens 'the rapist'; the fact that Couzens and other officers had shared racist, misogynistic and homophobic messages in a private WhatsApp group; the further allegations of indecent exposure.

When Couzens was sentenced after pleading guilty to all charges, the Met published guidance for women on how to protect themselves from police officers. Official advice included a suggestion that women in fear for their safety should resist arrest, refuse to be arrested until uniformed officers had arrived, run away from police or try to flag down a bus for assistance.[16]

Public statements released by the Met repeatedly referred to Couzens as an 'ex' or 'former' police officer.[17] But he was not an 'ex' police officer when he murdered Sarah Everard. Had he been an 'ex' police officer, he would not have had a warrant card. Had he been an 'ex' police officer, she might not have got into his car.

Couzens was not an anomaly: he was a symptom of a disease that has been spreading quietly throughout the police for some time.

In the last 12 years alone, 16 women have been murdered by current or former police officers in the UK.[18]

In March 2021 PC Oliver Banfield admitted attacking a woman in Warwickshire as she walked home alone at night. Using techniques taught to him as part of his police training, he grabbed her by the neck and wrestled her to the ground, calling her a 'fucking slag'. His victim suffered anxiety and panic attacks as a result of the assault, which she described as being 'terrifying' in itself, adding that 'to find out he was a police officer shook my belief system to its core'. Banfield resigned before a disciplinary hearing could be held. He did not go to prison and was sentenced to a curfew rather than a community order, as it would be 'difficult for him to work alongside criminals'.[19]

In November 2021 PC Jamie Rayner was jailed for two years and three months after being convicted of assaulting and strangling his partner – another police officer – during a coercive and controlling relationship. Rayner had intimidated his partner to the point where she was unable to tell friends or colleagues about his behaviour. The court heard evidence of messages he had sent her telling her how to lie about how her injuries were caused.[20]

In September 2021 Detective Inspector Neil Corbel, a serving Met officer, was convicted of 19 different offences of voyeurism against vulnerable women. Corbel served within the Continuous Policing Improvement Command unit, which is responsible for upholding professionalism and standards in policing.

Giving evidence in court, one of his victims said: 'It is particularly upsetting knowing he is a high-ranking police officer. I would expect far better from someone in his position.'

Another said: 'The fact that the defendant is a police officer has scared me and shocked me. He's supposed to enforce the law.'

A third said: 'If you can't trust police officers, then what are we supposed to do?'[21]

At Corbel's sentence hearing one of his victims said, 'I have pulled so much of my hair out with stress I have bald spots and have had to turn down work.' She showed the courtroom her scalp.

Corbel was sentenced to three years in prison.[22]

Serving officer Detective Constable Paul Allgood, who had previously been assigned to a specialist sex offences unit, was convicted in April 2021 of being in possession of indecent images of children and of outraging public decency. The court heard that the images seized included 32 of the most serious category, with some of the images depicting the abuse of babies. He had also 'upskirted' an unknowing schoolgirl, whose age was estimated at 13 or 14, on the London Underground. He received a suspended sentence.[23]

In June of 2021 Sergeant Benjamin McNish, who worked in a unit investigating child sexual abuse, was found guilty of filming a woman in the shower without her consent. He was given a suspended sentence.[24]

In January 2021 former sergeant Derek Seekings was convicted of two counts of rape, committed while he was a serving police officer, one of which took place while he was on duty. He was sentenced to 11 years in prison and placed on the sex offenders' register for life.[25]

In June 2020 PCs Deniz Jaffer and Jamie Lewis were ordered to attend the scene of a murder in a London park, where two sisters, Nicole Smallman and Bibaa Henry, had been stabbed to death. Instead of guarding the scene as ordered, they entered the crime scene and took photographs of the dead women. They circulated the photos in two separate WhatsApp groups, referring to the women as 'dead birds'. One of the WhatsApp groups contained 41 police officers. The other, a group made up of Jaffer's friends, was entitled 'Covid Cunts'. In November 2021 the officers pleaded guilty to misconduct in public office. The women's mother, Mina Smallman, told the court that the actions of the two officers had intensified the grief of the family – some of whom served in the Met themselves – and had robbed her daughters of dignity in death. Their actions also assisted the defence of the man eventually convicted of murdering Nicole and Bibaa, who argued at his trial that evidence obtained from the crime scene might have been contaminated by the two officers.[26] They were jailed for 33 months.

Police officer Alan Butler was convicted of two counts of misconduct in a public office in October 2021. He met one of his victims when she approached the police to report being abused by her adopted father when she was a child. While her allegations against her adopted father were being taken to trial, Butler manipulated her into a sexual relationship. As his victim put it, 'I trusted Alan, but in reality he was grooming and manipulating me to use me for his own sexual gratification.'[27] She added: 'Now, going back to relating it to what had happened with my adopted father, I could see that [Butler] was really doing the same thing.'[28] Butler was originally sentenced to 18 months in prison, but following a review by the Attorney General, the Court of Appeal deemed his sentence to be unduly lenient, and increased it to three years' imprisonment.[29]

These examples are all from 2021. They are all cases in which officers have been convicted of crimes. There are many more officers who have been accused of many more crimes since Couzens's conviction.

Not every case of police violence against women receives broad press coverage. Since 2017 there have been nearly 2,000 allegations of sexual misconduct against police officers, special constables and police community support officers.[30] The details of these allegations range from unwanted sexualised behaviour towards junior members of staff, to taking indecent photographs in the workplace, to an officer who used 'unreasonable force against his partner' on two separate occasions.[31]

In February 2022, details emerged of messages sent between Met officers based at Charing Cross Police Station. It was revealed that officers had joked about everything from rape to disabilities to sex offenders, in jokes that were homophobic, Islamophobic and openly racist. Then there was the misogyny. Below are just some of the text messages that were sent.

I fucking need to take my bird out, won't see her until next Saturday. Then I have to work. Promised to take her out the Friday after. Making it up to her from when I backhanded her

His colleague replied:

Grab her by the pussy

You ever slapped your missus? It makes them love you more. Seriously since I did that she won't leave me alone. Now I know why these daft cunts are getting murdered by their spastic boyfriends

Knock a bird about and she will love you. Human nature. They are biologically programmed to like that shit

Getting a woman into bed is like spreading butter. It can be done with a bit of effort using a credit card, but it's quicker and easier just to use a knife

My bird won't stop taking the piss. Swear to got [sic] I'm going to smack her

His colleague replied:

Slap her one... say you didn't

One officer was nicknamed 'Rapey McRaperson' because of his behaviour in 'harassing [women], getting on them, do you know what I mean being like, just a dick' and because of rumours he had brought a woman back to the police station for sex.

A female officer was told by colleagues, 'I would happily rape you' and 'If I was single I would happily chloroform you'.[32]

Not only did the officers feel comfortable expressing these opinions to colleagues but they were sure enough of the culture in which they operated that they put it in writing. That is not the behaviour of officers who think their views are at odds with the values of their organisation.

In 2021 researchers at Bournemouth University were given access to confidential files detailing 514 proven cases of sexual misconduct from 33 different police forces.

Their findings showed that:

- 20 per cent of women targeted by police officers had pre-existing mental health problems
- 25 per cent had suffered previous sexual assault
- 40 per cent were victims of previous domestic abuse.

As Dr Terri Cole, who conducted the research, observed: 'Sex offenders tend to target vulnerable victims, and we've found exactly the same in these types of [police] perpetrators. They tend to target victims of previous domestic violence, victims of sexual abuse, witnesses or victims that have had other trauma in their lives.'

Her colleague, Faye Sweeting, added: 'Officers are targeting people that they know maybe won't be believed, maybe won't be seen as credible, or who are more easily controllable, potentially.'[33]

Abuse of police power is not, therefore, simply a case of the occasional officer getting carried away. When we discuss sexual misconduct by police officers, we are not talking about a case of an officer bumping into someone while on duty, both feeling a spark, and a healthy and consensual relationship developing over time. It is the consistent and deliberate targeting of vulnerable victims who go to the police for help. It is the same pattern as has been observed in sex offenders.

The problem is not simply with police misconduct; it extends to how police officers are treated when their wrongdoing is uncovered. Between 2017 and 2020, more than half of the Met police officers who were found to have committed sexual misconduct kept their jobs.[34]

In October 2022, Baroness Casey published an interim report into misconduct within the Metropolitan Police. Its contents were deeply concerning, but not surprising. It gave the example of one officer who faced eleven separate allegations of wrongdoing including fraud, sexual harassment and assault. He continued to serve with the Met even after he was arrested for a sexual offence.[35]

Casey's report found evidence that fewer and fewer officers found guilty of gross misconduct are being dismissed as a result, leading to a lack of faith in police officers that the misconduct process works. The report noted: 'The experience that "nothing happens" when misconduct occurs dissuades officers and staff from reporting misconduct when they see it'.[36]

In March 2020, the Centre for Women's Justice submitted a super-complaint that exposed systemic failings in the way women were treated when reporting domestic abuse committed by police officers.[37] It reviewed 666 allegations of domestic abuse by police officers and revealed common themes experienced by victims. As well as difficulties in reporting the abuse in the first place, the report details consistent failings in the investigative process, including not reviewing supportive evidence, not speaking to witnesses and even asking one woman who reported her ex-husband, a police officer, 'if she would be happy to have her daughter interviewed and have her responsible for her father losing his job'.[38]

The super-complaint also included details of improper responses to complaints; allegations of domestic abuse by officers being 'investigated' by colleagues from the same police station, who know them personally; harassment of victims' new partners by other police officers; police abusers not being charged, despite independent supporting evidence; failure to instigate misconduct proceedings; employment and career difficulties for victims who are themselves police officers; and even the arrest of the abused women.[39]

In June 2022, Her Majesty's Inspectorate of Constabulary and Fire and Rescue Services (HMIC) responded to the CWJ super-complaint with a damning report. It found that just 9 per cent of reports of domestic abuse where the perpetrator was a police officer resulted in a suspect being charged. Having undertaken a detailed review of 56 separate investigations into such offences, it found that 22 of the investigations (39 per cent) were inadequate. Only 40 per cent of allegations of police-perpetrated domestic abuse resulted in an officer being investigated for misconduct. Perhaps not surprisingly given these findings, just under 6 per cent of women who reported police-perpetrated domestic abuse said they would feel confident to report it again.[40]

Public confidence in the police is essential for an effective and functioning justice system. Yet in October 2019, a YouGov poll found that more people are now unconfident (48 per cent) than confident (43 per cent) in the police's ability to deal with crime in their local area.[41] A further poll in November 2021 found that 47 per cent of women and 40 per cent of men said trust in police had decreased since the details of Wayne Couzens's crimes were made public. Just 29 per cent of women said they still trust the police despite Sarah Everard's murder.[42]

Women in Court

When the police do refer cases to the Crown Prosecution Service (CPS), the situation does not improve.

In 2020 the End Violence Against Women Coalition argued that the CPS had been prioritising conviction rates over the interests of justice, which one whistle-blower said resulted in 'the removal of hundreds of "weak" cases from the criminal justice system, which are less likely to find favour with a jury'. The whistle-blower stated that prosecutors were applying myths and stereotypes to rape cases and dropping them as a result.[1] Unpublished documents submitted to the government's Rape Review revealed that cases dropped by the CPS included one where the suspect's phone contained a video of the attack, and another where the alleged perpetrator had admitted to carrying out the offence in text messages. In one case, the reason not to charge a suspect was that the victim had 'enjoyed an adventurous sex life'.[2]

In June 2021 the government published its End-to-End Rape Review, which found that since 2016 there had been a 'significant decline' in the number of charges and prosecutions for rape cases, resulting in fewer convictions.[3] CPS annual figures showed that despite a slight increase in referrals from the police, the number of rape cases that reached court still fell by 25.9 per cent in the year 2020–2021.[4]

Discussing the review, Dame Vera Baird, the Victims' Commissioner, said, 'We are once more provided with yet further evidence – as if any more was needed – that the root of the problem lies at the door of the CPS.'[5]

Charges in rape cases are now half what they were in 2015–2016.[6] The data behind the End-to-End Rape Review found that CPS lawyers were taking around three times longer to make decisions about whether a suspect should be charged than they had in previous years.[7] Police officers stated that they believed the CPS would now only charge 'perfect' cases, and were trying to pre-empt jury decisions by not charging cases where there was a risk of not getting a conviction.[8] Some police officers claimed that the CPS decisions on whether or not to charge were informed by performance figures rather than by the evidence. One officer stated:

> They [CPS lawyers] are measured on attrition, so they'll only put through the ones that they know they are going to get conviction rates, so their conviction rates are quite high, but they're only putting – charging 3 per cent nationally, so they are getting [a] 2 per cent conviction rate, which is, you know – it just shows that they're not willing to take a chance on a wider range of cases.[9]

Police who participated in the rape review suggested that the CPS needed to make decisions more quickly, more consistently, and based on the evidence and the needs of the victim rather than internal targets. The CPS lawyers made similar suggestions for the police.

Whether the reason for the low number of successful prosecutions lies with the police or with the CPS, or (as seems likely) with both, it is self-evident that each branch blaming the other is not going to improve matters.

A review by the House of Commons Library in 2020 revealed that while the CPS caseload was becoming increasingly complex, CPS funding and staffing had fallen in recent years.[10] In 2018 the Justice Committee found poor performance by the CPS and deemed it to be a sign that the criminal justice system was 'under significant strain'.[11] While recent budgets increased the funding available to the CPS, the government has been warned that it is 'not enough to undo all the damage that has been done by years of cuts'.[12] A Channel 4 analysis demonstrated that, even with the increased government spending, applying inflation, the CPS has in fact suffered a real-term funding cut of 33 per cent over the last decade.[13]

Cuts to funding and limited staffing do not come close to excusing charging decisions based on myths and stereotypes rather than facts and evidence. But when budgets are cut, staffing is reduced and the pressure to achieve results remains, the inevitable outcome is one of poor decision-making, where CPS lawyers look for reasons not to prosecute, rather than ways to do it well.

The law has seen many positive changes in the treatment of people reporting violence, and particularly sexual violence, in recent years. Section 41 of the Youth Justice and Criminal Evidence Act 1999 provides that, where a person is charged with a sexual offence, the defence cannot introduce any evidence (including in cross-examination) about any previous sexual behaviour of the victim without express permission from the judge. The judge will only allow such evidence to be relied on in very narrow circumstances.

Section 36 of the same act allows judges to make an order preventing defendants who are representing themselves from cross-examining witnesses in certain cases. The rule is designed to stop the trial process from forming part of any abuse by ensuring that, even when defendants do not have legal representation for their whole trial, they are appointed a lawyer who undertakes cross-examination of the victim instead of them.[14] In 2021 the same rules were introduced to prevent abusers being able to cross-examine their victims in the family court and in civil proceedings.[15] While defendants are not able to cross-examine victims, however, they are still able to open and close their cases, cross-examine other witnesses, and put forward potentially abusive arguments without the benefit of legal advice and without adhering to the professional conduct rules that would bind a lawyer.

As detailed earlier in this section, at the end of trials for sexual assault judges routinely give directions to juries about the importance of ignoring stereotypes about what they imagine a victim's behaviour 'should' be like. This has a significant impact in shifting the emphasis of the defence in such cases: if a barrister knows that, after her closing speech, the judge will tell the jury to disregard stereotypes about rape, she is unlikely to rely on stereotypes about rape as part of her argument.

Victims of sexual offences are automatically entitled to special measures when giving evidence, as is any witness where their evidence is otherwise likely to be impacted by fear or distress.[16] These can include giving evidence from behind a screen or over video link to ensure that a victim does not have to see the defendant when they give their evidence. They can also include the removal of wigs and gowns so as to make the courtroom less intimidating for a witness, access to an intermediary and the provision of other aids to communication to help a witness give evidence.

Possibly the most significant development, however, is the ability to pre-record a witness's evidence prior to a trial. It is now routine that when a victim attends the police station to give an account of sexual violence, domestic abuse or any other offence that is likely to leave them vulnerable or intimidated, their interview is recorded. This recording then constitutes their evidence and is played, usually in edited form to remove inadmissible or irrelevant details, in court. More recently, video-recorded cross-examination has also been introduced for children and those affected by certain disabilities. Prior to trial, the victim attends court and is cross-examined by the defence barrister. This cross-examination is then recorded and played to the jury at a later date when the trial has started. The process is designed to minimise the number of times that a victim must tell their story, and to make the process of doing so less intimidating. It also has the added benefit that, if for some reason a trial has to be halted and re-started with a new jury, they do not have to go through giving evidence again.

Since 2016 barristers and solicitors have been able to undertake specialist training designed to assist with

vulnerable witnesses. The training focuses on the avoid-
ance of aggressive or crass questioning of witnesses as
well as signposting new topics to ensure that a witness is
able to answer questions properly, and involves careful
consideration of how to frame questions so as to properly challenge evidence without adding to any existing
trauma. While the course has been undertaken by over
3,000 lawyers, it is not yet compulsory.[17] His Honour
Peter Rook KC, an expert on the law and practice
surrounding sexual offences, pioneered the training and
has seen what he describes as a 'massive cultural change'
among barristers. There remains what he calls a 'pocket
of resistance among the rather older advocates, carrying
the baggage of the past 30 years' but notes that 'many
have embraced the changes'.[18]

Finally, the Domestic Abuse Act 2021 introduced two
new amendments that are likely to be of specific relevance to women who have suffered domestic abuse.
First, it created a new specific offence of strangulation or
suffocation. In a 2020 survey many victims of domestic
abuse reported being strangled by their abusers, who
used strangulation to instil fear in their victims, a large
number of whom said they genuinely believed they were
going to die.[19] Non-fatal strangulation is almost exclusively committed by men against women.[20] In the past,
the lack of physical marks left by strangulation meant
that the crime was seldom prosecuted, or, when it was, it

was prosecuted as a common assault – a much less serious offence.[21]

Secondly, the Domestic Abuse Act 2021 abolished the so-called 'rough sex defence', meaning that consent to serious harm for sexual gratification would no longer be a defence in law. The change followed a campaign from We Can't Consent to This, which found that at least 60 women had been killed by men who had relied on the defence in court.[22] The group found that in the last five years the defence was successful in 7 of 17 murder cases that went to trial, with the accused being either acquitted or being convicted of the lesser charge of manslaughter as a result.[23]

The cultural shift that coincided with the #MeToo movement has also made the legal system fairer for women. Better recognition of the realities of domestic abuse, rape and street harassment have not passed the legal system by and have certainly, in my experience, influenced the decision-making of judges. In a recent case, when defending a woman who was charged alongside her ex-partner with fraud, I argued that because of a history of abuse in the relationship their trials ought to be held separately. The judge initially described my argument as 'novel' – usually a death knell for any submission – but when we were able to produce an expert report highlighting how the abuse had affected my client and how it might impact on her ability to have a fair trial if she were to be beside him in the dock, the judge agreed and ordered two separate trials.

While improvements in certain areas have benefited women, where the system struggles is still women who are most deeply affected. There has been a growing backlog of criminal cases waiting to be tried since long before the Covid-19 pandemic. On 31 March 2019 the number of cases waiting to be tried in the Crown Court was 33,290. By 31 March 2020, it was 41,045.[24] The most recent figures available (November 2022) show an accumulation of almost 75,000 cases waiting to be heard – an increase of 55 per cent.[25] A report by the National Audit Office found that rape and serious sexual assault offences have been more acutely affected by the backlog than other cases, as a result of the fact that defendants accused of those offences are less likely to plead guilty than those in other cases.

As Kirsty Brimelow KC, vice-chair of the Criminal Bar Association, put it, 'Having seen – in certainly my early years of practice – how cases involving complainants in sexual offences would be expedited, now you're lucky if the case is heard within four years between complaint and trial.'

Brimelow explained that this means complainants 'just get fed up and they drop out of the system'. She added: 'It's a lot of stress; they want to move on with their lives.' This is an important factor to be aware of when considering reports of victims not supporting a prosecution: many do to begin with, but, having been told repeatedly that their case is delayed, they end up withdrawing their support.[26]

Talking to the BBC in December 2021, a victim of sexual abuse using the pseudonym of 'Alex' described the impact of the long delays in her case. The trial of her abuser has been repeatedly postponed since her case was first investigated in 2018.

> I'm trying to carry on a normal life, and I can't, it's just horrendous. It's like pretending to be someone else to live a normal life, to fit in a normal world. It's horrendous. I'm constantly thinking about it all the time. I'm having nightmares. I think I'm going to see [the defendant] and the doubt in my mind it's ever going to happen.

She described the significant impact on her mental health, stating that she'd had panic attacks while waiting for the trial to start.[27]

While the backlog had been a significant problem for some time before Covid-19, when the pandemic struck its impact was most keenly felt by the marginalised and the vulnerable. The National Audit Office report found that:

... the Ministry and HMCTS [Her Majesty's Courts and Tribunals Service] have a poor understanding of how the pandemic and recovery programme have affected vulnerable and ethnic minority users. Despite a series of commitments on supporting users who are vulnerable because of their age, mental disorders or physical impairment, we found slow progress in collecting data and evaluating evidence on how vulnerable users have been affected by, for example, remote access to justice.

We also found no evidence that the Ministry and HMCTS have any data on users' ethnicity to carry out meaningful analysis on whether ethnic minority groups have been disadvantaged by the pandemic or the recovery programme.[28]

One way in which Crown Courts appear to be trying to address the backlog is through increased use of 'floating' trials. A 'floater' is a trial that is not given a specific courtroom or judge, but which might be heard in any courtroom in a given court centre within a specific period of time – usually two weeks. These trials are designed to slot into courtrooms that suddenly become available when other trials do not go ahead – for example, because the defendant pleads guilty on the day of the trial, or when key witnesses are unable to attend through illness. Official guidance states that 'floating' trials should be reserved for cases that are short and uncomplicated, that involve few witnesses, and where the defendant is on bail. 'Floaters' that are not heard during their first window should be given priority over other cases in any future listing, and should only be given a 'floating' listing more than once in exceptional circumstances.[29] This is designed to recognise the need for certainty surrounding criminal trials for all involved, not least the defendant and witnesses.

When I began my career at the bar cases involving vulnerable witnesses, allegations of serious violence and sexual offences were all routinely given fixtures, meaning they were all but guaranteed to go ahead on the date planned. It was unthinkable ten years ago for a rape case to be given a 'floating' listing, for the very obvious and sensible reason that complainants in rape cases are likely to be extremely anxious about the trial, and so that anxiety would be only exacerbated by uncertainty about when their case is likely to be heard. A fixed date allows a complainant to prepare themselves properly for a trial. They can take the necessary time off work; they can ensure that they have family members or friends available to come with them to court; they can plan time off to recuperate afterwards. If they are in receipt of counselling, they can arrange appointments either side of the trial to allow them to prepare emotionally for the process of giving evidence, and to recover from it.

A 'floating' date allows none of these things. Instead, victims attend court and spend hours, sometimes days, waiting in a witness suite to find out if their case will go ahead. They routinely do not know until the day of their evidence whether or not they will have to go into the courtroom and discuss one of the most harrowing incidents of their life. Often, having reached the point where they are ready, they are then told that their case cannot be heard. They will have to come back. The next available listing is in nine months. Their case is likely to be heard then, but the court cannot make any promises.

A report from the Victims' Commissioner found that concerns about the criminal justice process was the most common reason given by victims for withdrawing their allegations of serious sexual violence, affecting 26 per cent of people, while 13 per cent expressed fear that involvement in the criminal justice system would negatively affect their mental health.[30]

While much has been done to safeguard women in general when they attend court, once again marginalised women seem not to have been considered as fully. A 2021 report found that only 2 per cent of UK courts are currently fully accessible to disabled people, with only 16 per cent fully accessible for wheelchair users.[31] For disabled women attending court to give evidence about a crime they have suffered, the process of finding the courage to come to court only to then have to deal with barriers that prevent them from being able to use the building is unlikely to make their court experience any easier. Likewise, while Crown Courts are now routinely set up to prevent prosecution witnesses bumping into defendants in the corridors, in other courts this is not always the case. A client of mine recently gave evidence at the disciplinary hearing of a police officer charged with sexual misconduct against her, only to have him walk past her in full uniform and in the company of other police officers in the corridor of the court. Understandably, she felt tremendously intimidated.

In my experience the vast majority of barristers defending allegations of violence against women behave impeccably towards those making the allegations. There are, unfortunately, some notable exceptions.

In March 2015, Michael Magarian KC was defending one of five men charged with multiple child-sex offences committed against girls aged 13-16, arising out of a 'grooming ring' in Oxfordshire. In his closing speech, he referred to the case as a 'witch-hunt' that had been 'police manufactured'. Expanding on why (according to his client) the girls had fabricated the allegations, he concluded, 'It's better to be a victim than a slag.' He added: 'Once you are a victim who has been groomed, you no longer have to take responsibility for anything that you did.'[32] The Bar Standards Board records show no disciplinary findings against Mr Magarian KC.

In 2017 Howard Godfrey KC, when representing a man who had been convicted of sexually abusing his step-daughter, made similar remarks about the victim when appearing in front of the Court of Appeal to argue for a reduction in his client's sentence. He described his client's victim as 'not a young innocent girl, and I say it with all due respect'.

He was interrupted by one of the Court of Appeal judges, who clarified: 'He was looking after a child, and he gave her alcohol and then abused her.'

Mr Godfrey KC responded: 'My Lord, I do not think it is a case of – this girl was not unaccustomed to drinking. The family –'

He was interrupted by one of the other Court of Appeal judges, who commented: 'I must say, Mr Godfrey, I think attacking the victim is not necessarily going to be a very profitable exercise for you.'

Mr Godfrey was formally reprimanded and ordered to attend a training course on Advocacy and the Vulnerable in 2017.[33]

In 2015 barrister David Thomas Osborne wrote a blog about cases where drunk women were raped, saying:

I have a very simple solution which I hope you will agree is fair. If the complainant (I do not refer to her as the victim) was under the influence of alcohol or drugs, or both, when she was 'raped', this provides the accused with a complete defence. End of story and a victory for fairness, moderation and common sense![34]

He was roundly criticised but defended himself in media interviews, saying that rape statistics would fall if women who 'trollop around with their tits out' stopped getting 'legless' and 'covered up'.[35] He remains in practice from his own chambers in Somerset.[36] The Bar Standards Board records show no disciplinary findings against him in respect of the blog.

To mis-speak in court is an easy thing to do; all barristers do it at some point, and most immediately correct themselves. To mis-speak in such a way as to blame a victim for her own assault in (one assumes) a carefully planned closing speech, or in front of the Court of Appeal, is perhaps a little more revealing of an attitude than a slip of the tongue. To write an entire blog post promoting a change to the law that would mean women cannot drink any alcohol without this legally amounting to consent to sexual activity with literally anyone is absurd, dangerous and deeply damaging to the reputation of barristers everywhere.

Reports of incidents like these all have an impact on public confidence in the courts system. If a victim of serious violence cannot be assured that she will not be blamed, shamed or belittled by officers of the court in which she is giving evidence, is it surprising that so many are reluctant to do so?

For the most serious cases, no matter what the investigation and trial process might entail, it is a jury that makes the final decision. The question of whether juries 'work' is a complex one and the body of theory and research too large to be condensed into a book of this size. Part of the difficulty in knowing the extent to which jury biases impact on the fairness of the judicial system is that, unlike in the US, we do not permit jurors to be interviewed after a trial. This arguably assists with fairer decision-making, since jurors are able to remain anonymous and know that they will not be subjected to public pressure for making a decision that might be unpopular. However, the inability to consistently establish reasons for a jury's decision-making means it is possible that juries reach decisions based on factual inaccuracies, misunderstanding or misapplication of the law, or personal biases. Indeed, repeated studies using mock trials have convincingly established that juries are susceptible to false and prejudicial beliefs about rape, from what constitutes rape, to the expected behaviour of 'genuine' rape victims.[37]

Since jurors are drawn from the general population, a jury is likely to have many of the same characteristics that we find in society as a whole, including the same prejudices and bigotries that we know are widely prevalent. The prospect of getting an entirely unbiased jury is slim, hence the judicial directions on things like disregarding myths or stereotypes about how we might expect victims of sexual violence to behave. However, research has shown that 'juror education', whether through instructions from a judge or by way of expert evidence, can have a significant impact on a juror's decision-making.[38] While juries are far from perfect, they remain the least flawed option for determining something as serious as criminal guilt.

There is another side to jurors being representatives of society, however, and it denotes a perverse benefit of the overwhelming ubiquity of violence against women. If 71 per cent of women have experienced street harassment, and a jury is made up of 12 people, then it is likely that at least a few people on your jury know how it feels.[39] If one in three women experiences domestic abuse in her lifetime, then statistically at least two jurors might have.[40] I am not suggesting for a moment that these women are obliged to share their experiences with other jurors, but the jury process is designed to ensure that their voices are heard during the process of deliberation. And any thoughtful barrister will be mindful of the fact that, when addressing a jury, they are statistically likely to be addressing a victim of gender-based violence. An intelligent barrister will use that knowledge to inform their approach. Only a stupid one would try to persuade a jury with victim-blaming.

Victims of a violent or sexual crime whose attacker is sentenced to 12 months or more in prison are eligible to join the Victim Contact Scheme. People who do so are then given a Victim Liaison Officer, who will keep them informed as to the offender's release date, how to have input into parole-board hearings and how to apply for licence conditions to stop the offender from doing certain things on release (such as making contact with them). However, women who do not meet these criteria are left to learn in other ways what has happened to the offender. Nicola Brookes, who was stalked for over a year, only found out from friends that her stalker had been released early from prison.[41]

The longer-term impact on victims of gender-based violence is complex. I have had many clients who have ended up on trial themselves because of the impact of domestic abuse, and in particular coercive control. Perversely, while the law now recognises coercive control as a crime in itself, thereby acknowledging the power that abuse can exercise over a woman's actions, being subjected to coercive control cannot provide a defence for an abused woman who was pressured or intimidated into committing or assisting with criminal acts. In one case, my client was charged with perjury for putting her boyfriend's name on the birth certificate of her oldest child, even though the pair had not yet met when the child was born. My client had nothing to gain from lying on a birth certificate, and text messages later revealed that he had pressured her to do it out of a desire to erase any trace of other men from her life. The CPS eventually discontinued the prosecution against her, but only after she had been arrested at work, detained in a police cell away from her children and had attended court for three separate hearings.

In my experience, police officers' ability to recognise abuse can vanish when a woman defends herself. A client of mine, 'Keira', had been in an abusive relationship with her husband for a number of years. Records showed that he had multiple convictions for violence against her, and there was one allegation of Keira being violent to him. I met her in a cell at court, charged with attempted murder after she had stabbed her husband. Eventually, she explained that she and her husband had argued and, drunk, he had repeatedly hit her head with a hammer. She had grabbed the nearest thing – a small kitchen knife – and stabbed him until he stopped. She had then run out into the street, where the police had found her. She was 24 weeks pregnant.

She pleaded not guilty on the basis of self-defence. Before the trial we obtained disclosure of, among other things, her medical records. They showed that, on the only other occasion she had been accused of being violent to her husband, Keira had also been pregnant. She later told me, 'I can take it when it's just me. But not the baby.'

The pre-trial disclosure also revealed that, at the house, police had found a hammer. Forensic analysis showed it was covered with Keira's blood, Keira's hair and her husband's fingerprints.

Outside of court I raised all these points with the barrister prosecuting the case, who was entirely sympathetic, but he was nevertheless told by the CPS to proceed with the trial. I was able to persuade the judge to stop the trial at the halfway mark on a technical legal point. The case was dismissed and Keira released.

Keira had spent six months in prison waiting for her trial. She gave birth in prison. Her baby was taken from her.

57 per cent of women in prison are survivors of domestic violence.

53 per cent experienced emotional, physical or sexual abuse as a child.

Women's imprisonment results in an estimated 17,240 children being separated from their mothers every year.[42]

Part Three

HOW TO END IT

Political Will

In recent years a wealth of proposals that would make a positive change for women have been refused by those with the power to implement them.

The Centre for Women's Justice (CWJ), a legal charity that specialises in challenging discrimination against women and girls in the justice system, recommended two amendments to what became the Domestic Abuse Act 2021. The first built on the principle of the so-called 'householder defence', where the law grants more leeway to a person who acts in self-defence when confronted with a burglar in their home than it does to people in other situations, entitling them to use force that might be deemed disproportionate. The CWJ proposed extending this defence to circumstances where a victim of domestic abuse uses 'disproportionate' force to defend themselves from their abuser.

The second amendment advocated by the Centre for Women's Justice built on the defence that already exists under the Modern Slavery Act 2015, which acknowledges that victims of trafficking might be forced to commit crimes as a result of being trafficked. The CWJ proposed extending the defence to those who were victims of coercive and controlling relationships.

Neither of these two changes would allow a victim of domestic abuse to behave in any way they chose with impunity. They would simply provide legal recognition of that which is known by experts and was even recognised by the government when it made coercive control a crime: that domestic abuse can be so powerful as to diminish a person's responsibility for their actions. The implementation of these defences would have gone some way to undermining the stereotype of the 'ideal victim' that pervades society, as well as providing a fairer and more balanced system of justice that better served the people worst affected by abuse.

Both amendments were approved by the House of Lords. The government rejected them.[1]

As part of the House of Lords debate on the Police, Crime, Sentencing and Courts Bill, an amendment was proposed that would establish a Women's Justice Board. The board would consist of between 10 and 12 people with extensive recent experience of women and the justice system, and would have a range of powers (including commissioning research) to support women in the justice system. The amendment was rejected by the House of Lords.[2]

The definition of hate crime currently extends to those targeted on the basis of their race, religion, disability, sexual orientation or transgender identity.[3] Hate crimes legislation allows prosecutors to apply for an increased sentence for a person who commits one. It is designed to recognise the particularly poisonous harm that comes from being a victim of a crime not at random, but because of who you are. If one person targets another based on their sex or gender, there is no hate crime recorded. There is no increased sentence. From 2016, 11 police forces around the country have been trialling recording misogyny as a hate crime. Senior police officers have backed the idea, saying it would be 'a welcome addition to how we respond to crime and behaviour in this area'.[4] Boris Johnson ruled out the possibility, claiming that to record misogyny as a hate crime would overload the police.[5] Violence against women is seemingly such a prolific problem that the government has decided to do nothing about it.

On 17 January 2022 the House of Lords voted in favour of an amendment to the Police, Crime, Sentencing and Courts Bill to make misogyny a hate crime. The amendment was proposed by Baroness Newlove, a Conservative peer and former Victims' Commissioner.[6] The government rejected it.

The problem is not a lack of ideas for how to end violence against women or improve women's experience of the justice system when they suffer violence; the problem is a lack of political will.

The definition of misogyny is 'hatred, dislike, or mistrust of women, manifested in various forms such as physical intimidation and abuse, sexual harassment and rape, social shunning and ostracism, etc'.[7] Its male equivalent is misandry.[8] Feminism is 'the belief in social, economic, and political equality of the sexes'.[9]

In an interview with BBC *Breakfast* about crimes against women, Dominic Raab MP said, 'Misogyny is, of course, absolutely wrong, whether it's a man against a woman or a woman against a man.'[10] When asked in 2019 whether he would describe himself as a feminist, he replied, 'No, probably not.'[11] He had previously described feminists as 'amongst the most obnoxious bigots' and, when given an opportunity to reconsider that position, defended it.[12] In 2021 he was appointed Minister for Justice. He was reinstated to that post by Rishi Sunak in 2022.

Raab's track record suggests that ending violence against women is far from the top of his agenda. Yet more concerning still is the potential impact of his intention to abolish the Human Rights Act, replacing it with a so-called Bill of Rights, which could do real harm to women, and especially to the ability of women to get justice when they are failed by public authorities.

For policy reasons, it is extremely difficult to sue the police for negligence. So for women who suffer serious sexual violence and are let down by the police, often their only hope of justice lies with the Human Rights Act, which guarantees women a right to have their allegations properly investigated by the police. For the women I represent – whose allegations of rape are ignored, belittled or laughed at – the Human Rights Act is often the only way they can hold the police to account.

The plans to abolish these rights would be concerning in any circumstances. But the government openly states that one of the aims of the Bill of Rights is 'reducing unnecessary litigation and avoiding undue risk aversion for bodies delivering public services'.[13] In other words, the plan is not only to abolish one of the few rights to redress that women have against the police: Raab's proposals would aim to make it harder still for women to get justice. His description of himself as 'probably not' a feminist seems to be terrifyingly accurate.

A recent Law Commission report recommended creating a new crime of public sexual harassment, while simultaneously acknowledging that there are already laws in place that address much of the behaviour we associate with street harassment.[14] It outlined that the benefit of a specific offence of public sexual harassment was that it 'might be crafted in a way that better captures the degrading and sexualised nature of the behaviour' of harassment of women.[15]

It is already illegal to behave in public in a threatening or abusive way that is likely to cause a person harassment, alarm or distress. It has been since the Public Order Act 1986 came into effect.

It is already a crime to pursue a course of conduct that amounts to the harassment of another. It has been since the Protection from Harassment Act 1997 came into effect.

It could be argued that, despite these crimes already existing, there is a potential benefit to new legislation designed to specifically address street harassment. Like a new year's resolution, a new criminal offence can improve things in the short term: it makes offenders more aware that they are breaking the law, victims more aware that they can report it to the police, and police officers more likely to record it.[16] But, just like a new year's resolution, it doesn't last.

The problem is not that we don't have the laws to combat gender-based violence; it's that we don't use them. And if we're not using the ones we have, what point is there in making more?

How to Make the Police Safe for Women

In recent years the police has faced a barrage of funding cuts, with central grants falling by 30 per cent in real terms between 2010 and 2019.[1] As a result, police forces have increasingly had to rely on their financial reserves – a finite pool of money set aside for unforeseeable or emergency spending. The most recent data available shows that 88 per cent of forces are relying on reserve funding to finance day-to-day operations.[2] As well as relying on reserves, police forces have also had to sell off assets, including police stations, to raise money. Between 400 and 600 police stations were closed between 2010 and 2018.[3] It is not, perhaps, surprising that among this crisis of resources 40 per cent of police forces do not even have specialist units for dealing with rape and serious sexual offences.[4]

There is evidence to suggest that demands on the police are increasing, in part as a result of a rise in complex crimes that are more challenging for the police to respond to.[5] Despite these factors, 64 per cent of police time is spent on non-crime-related incidents, such as road traffic accidents, mental health incidents and missing person's cases.[6] The 'Defund the Police' movement, centred in the US, advocates diverting funds from police departments to non-policing forms of community support and public safety, including mental health services, youth services, housing and social services. In the UK, however, a lack of resources for police, combined with a lack of funding for other crucial community support, is arguably precisely the source of the problem. The absence of resources for proper mental health care means police are often the last safety net for those suffering mental health crises.[7] This puts officers in a position where they are responding to situations outside of their expertise, and which can take a considerable amount of time to resolve, leading to a lack of capacity to deal with crime.[8]

In these circumstances, evidence of police failings when dealing with crimes against women and girls should be no surprise: even the best officers, when placed under the sort of pressure currently facing the police, are likely to struggle. The primary response to the epidemic of violence against women must be to properly fund and train those who police it.

Police officers themselves have complained that they are not routinely receiving the training they need to properly respond to, investigate and prevent violence against women.[9] A fundamental part of the change required to end the culture of violence against women is to properly train police officers to investigate it. The training must be mandatory, and it must include, as a minimum:

- the prevalence of violence against women;
- barriers to reporting, including why women might distrust the police;
- sensitivity training in dealing with victims;
- what lesser crimes are available to be prosecuted, including coercive and controlling behaviour, stalking, harassment, public order offences, disclosing images without consent, malicious communications and misuse of the public communications network. Evidence suggests that these 'smaller' offences can be an early indicator of more serious criminal behaviour towards women, yet experience shows they are routinely under-charged;[10]
- and, crucially, how to properly investigate crimes against women, including:
  > that the focus should be on the perpetrator, not on the victim;
  > that there is no reason in fact or in law why a prosecution cannot go ahead based on the word of one person alone;
  > how to properly read forensic reports.

Finally, and perhaps most importantly, all police training should encompass the specific problems faced by marginalised women, and how to best support those experiencing them.

In 2021 Sistah Space launched a campaign for 'Valerie's Law', named after Valerie Forde.[11] The proposed law would make it compulsory for all police officers, and other agencies that support black women and girls affected by domestic abuse, to have training to facilitate a better understanding of the cultural needs of black women. A petition for Valerie's Law received over 106,000 signatures before it closed. The government responded that it has no plans to implement it.[12]

The status quo is unacceptable. It is unacceptable that a blind woman was told that police could not prosecute allegations of sexual assault on public transport – rife with CCTV – because she 'cannot identify her perpetrators'.[13] It is unacceptable that police officers made judgments about the inherent worth of child victims of sexual assault, concluded that they should have been 'drowned at birth', and used that as a reason not to proceed with an investigation. It is unacceptable that darker-skinned black women are disbelieved because their skin does not show bruising as clearly as that of lighter-skinned women. It is unacceptable that the most marginalised women in society receive less protection from the police, not more.

This is not an exercise in ticking diversity boxes. It is not about being performatively kind. It is about the fact that, as things stand, the police are only serving part of the country – and it is not the part that needs them the most.

Police officers are drawn from an unfair and unequal society that already discriminates against marginalised women. That is not an excuse for the police to reflect those problems. Nor is the lack of resources an excuse for the police to perform as poorly as they are when it comes to protecting women. Police officers should be the standard bearers for proper conduct, working to make the country fairer, not exacerbating the discriminations and disadvantages that exist in wider society. Police are often the last line of defence for vulnerable women: they should be held to a higher standard, not a lower one.

There are innumerable other proposals for improving the performance of the police in investigating and preventing crimes against women. While many of these provide sticking plasters, none will be effective in any meaningful way without significant, lasting and nation-wide cultural change in the police.

The resignation of Cressida Dick provided many with hope that her successor would bring change to the Met. I was less optimistic. Everything we know about cultural change suggests that those who rise to the top of an organisation are the least likely to want to transform it as a result. If you do well in a police force that is culturally misogynistic, it is unlikely that you are the right person to end misogyny within the police.

Sir Mark Rowley, appointed as Dame Cressida's replacement in September 2022, had previously been the Chief Constable of Surrey Police before serving in the Met as Acting Deputy Commissioner. Discussing the findings of the Casey report in an interview with LBC, Sir Mark said that he had never seen or heard of the conduct exposed in the Casey report but was determined to 'sort it'.[14]

Whistle-blower after whistle-blower has called out the culture of toxic misogyny in police forces up and down the country.

Sue Fish, the former chief constable of Nottingham Police, responded to the murder of Sarah Everard by saying, 'This isn't about an individual officer. This is about a prevailing culture within policing and it has to be broken. It had to have been broken many years ago.'[15]

Former Chief Superintendent Parm Sandhu has called the Met 'very sexist and misogynistic'. She has also observed how difficult it is for female officers to call out the behaviour of their colleagues:

What happens is that male police officers will then close ranks and the fear that most women police officers have got is that when you are calling for help, you press that emergency button on your radio, they're not going to turn up and you're going to get kicked in in the street.[16]

In 2019, then Met Detective Superintendent Paige Kimberley reported a police WhatsApp group containing 'serious misogyny' to her manager, which resulted in her having an offer of a new job withdrawn.[17]

Janet Hills MBE, former chair of London's Black Police Association, said 'There needs to be zero tolerance [for sexism] and there isn't. There is this sort of leeway of "Oh well it was just a joke or bants or whatever". It's then not recorded, and therefore the behaviours increase and get worse'.[18]

Nogah Ofer, a solicitor at the Centre for Women's Justice, has expressed concern about 'a "locker-room culture" that trivialises violence against women, where loyalty towards fellow officers and concern about impact on their careers may be getting in the way of justice for women who report abuse'.[19]

We are seeing a growing body of evidence that the police is institutionally misogynistic. As long as that remains the case, the best initiatives in the world will not improve the situation for women.

The current disciplinary process is not fit for ridding the police of misogynistic officers, or for bolstering public confidence in the idea that police culture is changing. If the police wishes to have any hope of restored credibility, a complete revision of the disciplinary process is vital. There must be a zero-tolerance approach to officers who display sexism and misogyny.

The culture you get is the behaviour you tolerate. The status quo cannot continue.

For change to be effective it must be not just reactive, but preemptive. From the beginning of the police recruitment process, recruiters must be focused on identifying and removing prospective officers who demonstrate violent and damaging attitudes to women. The emphasis on identifying and removing misogyny must continue throughout new-recruit training and in all subsequent areas of police training and work. Training in policing violence against women must be mandatory, rigorous and frequent. Communication between police forces must be standardised and improved to ensure that if, as Wayne Couzens did, an officer transfers between different police forces, 'red flag' behaviour is not allowed to slip through the cracks. There must be no safe place for misogyny in the police.

We cannot seriously tell ourselves that the police is spearheading action to end violence against women when more than half of Met officers found guilty of sexual misconduct keep their jobs.[20] We cannot expect the public to accept that the police is taking violence against women seriously when there is so much evidence of it being police officers themselves who commit it. We cannot say in good conscience that the police is efficiently holding itself accountable when officers accused of domestic violence are routinely investigated by their own colleagues.[21] We cannot honestly claim that the police is working well for women when those who are afraid they might be murdered by a police officer are told, by the then head of the Metropolitan Police herself, to 'flag down a bus'.[22]

The answer from Dame Cressida Dick, when asked what women could do to make themselves safe from police officers, should have been 'nothing'.

When police officers are not just failing to properly investigate crimes against women, but are committing them themselves, it is too late for sticking plasters. Real, significant and lasting change is needed in the police if there is to be any hope of addressing the flood of violence against women and girls. Change to funding, change to training and change to culture. It must be revolutionary, it must be top to bottom, and it must start now.

A System of Justice

The justice system cannot deliver on a shoestring. As long as there is a shortage of resources, there will be pressure to abandon cases. As long as there is that pressure, there will be those relying on myths, stereotypes and victim-blaming as a result. A properly resourced Crown Prosecution Service is vital if we ever hope to see the conviction rates for crimes against women increase. It is farcical for the government to criticise the CPS for not prosecuting more cases while simultaneously denying them the funds to do it.

The CPS has excellent guidance on the prosecution of offences against women, available online for all to see. It has thorough and detailed sections on tackling rape myths, dealing with domestic abuse allegations and supporting vulnerable victims through the court process. But between the written guidance and those tasked with implementing it, there has been a breakdown. The CPS cannot claim to be tackling rape myths in court while its lawyers write off a prosecution because the complainant 'enjoyed an adventurous sex life'.[1] The guidance must be embedded in the culture of the CPS, and lawyers held accountable when it is not.

Needless to say, it is not just prosecutors who must appreciate the complexity of issues surrounding violence against women if the justice system is to improve. The need for education, training and understanding extends to all those who work within the criminal justice system, including defence practitioners. The examples of Michael Magarian KC, Robert Colover, Howard Godfrey KC and David Osborne are all painful evidence of what happens when that understanding is lacking. The fact that only Howard Godfrey KC faced a sanction of any kind is concerning. The conduct of these men, and of others like them, is unacceptable. It undermines public confidence in the justice system and undoubtedly contributes to the problem of women who are victims of serious violence not wanting to go to court. It is not proper behaviour. Happily, in my experience, it is less and less common.

Some time ago, I was instructed to defend an allegation of sexual assault where my client's defence was that no sexual activity had occurred between him and his accuser. Consent was not in issue and could not have had less bearing on the case. Before the trial my instructing solicitor sent me a series of WhatsApp messages containing photographs of the complainant in her underwear and told me to put them before the jury. The photos had no relevance whatsoever to the issue in the case. Their only purpose would be to humiliate and shame the complainant. I refused. Colleagues to whom I have relayed this story – male and female, and of all political persuasions – have been universally horrified at the solicitor's behaviour. The solicitor himself has not sent me a case since. I have lost no sleep over it.

From time to time people appear in the media to attack lawyers who defend those charged with violence against women. The lawyers are rhetorically asked how it is that they can cross-examine victims; how they can sleep at night knowing that they defend rapists for a living. The logic behind this argument eludes me. Is the suggestion that any person is guilty of any crime of which they are accused, regardless of what the evidence shows? Is the suggestion that democracy requires a fair trial for all, except those charged with crimes against women? There are many brilliant feminist lawyers who defend people charged with serious sexual violence for a living. They are precisely the people who *should* be defending those trials. They challenge the evidence properly and legitimately. They make sure that the accused has a fair trial, and that any conviction is a safe one. But in doing so they do not pander to myths about female behaviour that are not only outdated, but demonstrably false. It is these lawyers, above all others, who are bringing the justice system up to date. We need more of them.

That any complainant would prefer to be cross-examined by a feminist barrister is obvious. But any defendant would also be wise to ask a feminist to represent him. Given the strong probability of a jury containing one or more person who has experienced some form of gender-based violence, a barrister who shames, derides or attacks a complainant has not helped their client at all.

While training on Advocacy and the Vulnerable has been taken by many barristers, it is not compulsory – and experience shows that, as with a lot of voluntary training, those who need it most are the least likely to take it. For public confidence, and for justice to be done, training on violence against women (including the compounded discrimination faced by marginalised women) ought to be mandatory for barristers.

A more representative justice system is also vital to ensure not just public confidence, but also fair treatment of women. As things stand, women make up just 32.4 per cent of police officers, 37 per cent of CPS advocates and 32 per cent of judges;[2] 92.7 per cent of police officers, 70 per cent of CPS advocates and 93 per cent of judges are white.[3] Just under 2 per cent of police officers and 11 per cent of CPS advocates declared themselves to have a disability – there were no statistics available for judges.[4] While the human ability to empathise is a cornerstone of the justice system, it cannot seriously be argued that it is a substitute for the life experience and breadth of thought that comes from real representation. A more representative justice system is a fairer justice system. It is also a more credible one.

While the instruction to juries to disregard rape myths and stereotypes has been well received, it is not clear why the justice system has chosen to stop at rape. Harmful myths pervade all aspects of violence against women, with those surrounding domestic abuse being perhaps the most pervasive. It is vital that, in assessing evidence of domestic abuse, juries are given a basic level of understanding about the ways in which abuse can affect people. Without it, there remains the risk that, at the end of the trial, 12 people retire to their jury room and ask, 'If it was so bad, why didn't she leave?' There is no good reason in fact or law why juries cannot be instructed by a judge to ignore myths and stereotypes about domestic abuse in the same way as they are told to ignore myths and stereotypes about rape. It is a basic step towards a better-informed jury that could go a long way to ensuring a fairer justice system.

One of the best ways to change the legal system is to use it. Since 2013, the Victims' Right to Review scheme has provided victims of crime with an automatic process to appeal when police or the CPS decide not to prosecute.[5] It is also possible in some circumstances to bring a civil case against the police for failing to properly investigate allegations of serious violence. Yet in my experience many women do not know that these avenues are available to them, and those who do are, understandably, often too exhausted by their own trauma to consider legal action.

Women who use the law to hold the justice system to account are rarely doing it just for themselves. Without exception, the women I represent are driven by a desire not just to achieve justice in their own cases, but to prevent what happened to them from happening again to other women. Their litigation is a public service, but one that, thanks to the devastating cuts to legal aid, many pay for out of their own pocket. Those without a source of private funds are often left without recourse to justice. Once more, in this fight, marginalised women are left behind.

In short, the justice system has much room for improvement, and the changes needed are simple and self-evident: better funding, better training, cultural change and real access to justice even for those who cannot afford it.

Cultural Change: The Disease and the Symptom

The solution to the problem of violence against women and girls is not, however, solely a question of fixing the police, fixing the Crown Prosecution Service or fixing the courts. That is clear for two reasons. First, the police, the CPS and the courts are all there to provide a response to violence against women. In theory, the police also deals with prevention, but the common reality is that all three can only deal with the aftermath. And what comes next is rarely justice – not just because of how low conviction rates are, but because in all the years I have been doing this job, in all the positive outcomes I have had, I have never been able to give a single client what they really want: the ability to turn back time and stop the crime from ever happening. The courts can clear up the site of the disaster, put the furniture back and try to make it look like it did before. They can reinforce some structures to try to stop it happening again. But, too often, that is as far as justice can go.

Secondly, the police, the CPS and the courts are populated by human beings. As long as there is space within society for a person to think, 'She's asking for it'; for them to shout sexual abuse at a teenage girl in the street; to slide a hand onto the knee of a junior colleague under the desk; to grab at a woman jogging past – as long as there is space for that person to exist in society, there is space for that person to be a police officer. To be a lawyer. To be a juror. To be a judge.

Misogyny walks among us every day in plain clothes. It is in the men who come home carrying flowers for their broken wives, promising it'll be different this time. It is in the women who read a report of a woman attacked in the street and think, 'What was she doing by herself in the middle of the night?' It is in those who laugh off rape jokes; who pretend not to hear; who won't look up; who don't intervene. It is in every one of us who stands by.

To have any hope of ending violence against women, we must first know what the problem is. To ensure that our response is fair and serves everyone, we need to pay attention to everybody. With so many marginalised women excluded from the data, that is impossible. Rather than revealing the extent and variety of the problems faced, the data shines a light on 'women generally', ignoring the darker corners where gender intersects with race and disability and sexuality and class.

Where the statistics do include marginalised women, they reveal compounded cruelty. So, for the statistics that are not there, what more might we be missing? We use the term 'just another statistic' to refer to people who are written off without being given due consideration, but for marginalised women, they are not even given the dignity of being a statistic in the first place.

The Crime Survey for England and Wales has an age cap of 74, and excludes those in care homes and refuges, meaning that if a woman of 75 is murdered, her death does not count towards crime statistics.[1] In 79 per cent of homicide cases the ethnicity of the victim is not recorded, meaning we can't reliably assess any racial disparities across the victims of violent crime – or any changes in that dynamic over time.[2] At every turn, when researching this book, specific data on marginalised women was missing. Where data was present it was most commonly sourced through the arduous and unreliable process of Freedom of Information Act requests by non-profit organisations.

If we cannot identify what the problem is, we have no hope of fixing it. We cannot continue to rely on charitable organisations to spend their limited resources on compiling data. The Office for National Statistics, the Crime Survey for England and Wales, and all other major data sources have to be routinely asking for a breakdown of data to show the ways in which specific problems affect specific women. Failing to do so makes statistics a blunt tool that prioritises the most visible and further disadvantages those who most need to be seen.

In a world where the harvesting of data can predict everything from what adverts we like to whether or not we are pregnant, it is nothing short of offensive that we do not have the most basic data available on the violence against marginalised women.[3] We must abolish the age cap on the Crime Survey for England and Wales. We must include women in refuges in our statistics. When statistics are collated, they must include breakdowns by ethnicity, by socio-economic status, by religion, by LGBTQ+ identity and by disability. Where experience shows us certain groups are likely to experience discrimination, we must investigate the statistical data to confirm it and, more importantly, to treat it. We must make that data available freely to those who need to see it so they can best help the women who need it most.

The failure to recognise the specific needs of marginalised women in statistical analysis is reflected in our failure to provide specialist services for marginalised women in the community. It is insincere to suggest that we as a society care for all women if we are not providing women-only homeless shelters for those who, fleeing violence, are terrified to be housed with men. It is inconsistent to argue that we are an equal society if the only specialist centres for women who have suffered FGM are in Bristol, Birmingham, Leeds and London, hundreds of miles away from many of the women who need them.[4] It is hollow to state that we care about the trans community when trans women escaping domestic abuse are frequently refused a bed in a refuge.[5] It is laughable to claim that we respect the dignity of disabled women when they are disproportionately at risk of all forms of violence. It is simply wrong to say that we value women of all ethnicities equally when domestic abuse services specifically for women of colour survive on less money and are more likely to close.[6]

To have any hope of ending violence against women, we cannot continue to treat it as a flat problem that affects all women equally. It does not. As long as our reporting, resources and advocacy fail to reflect that, we are part of the problem.

Perhaps the biggest misconception about violence against women is that it is about women at all. It is not. The violence towards women overwhelmingly comes from men. It is male violence that is the problem. And the victims of male violence are not just women.

We are a society that is still just a few decades on from horrific wars that devastated a generation of men and told them to keep silent about it. That told them violence was noble, and that any emotional fallout from it was undignified. And that watched as they taught their sons the same thing.

In a 2018 study, 61 per cent of 18-24-year-old men said they felt compelled to display 'hyper-masculine' behaviour in difficult situations, while 55 per cent said crying in front of others made them feel like 'less of a man', and 53 per cent felt that society expects men never to ask for emotional support, even when they need it.[7]

Is it surprising, then, in a society that still teaches men that crying isn't manly but violence is, that men's suicide rate is three times that of women?[8] Or that 85 per cent of violent crimes are committed by men?[9]

A fundamental part of addressing violence against women is tackling the violence of men, at every stage, and in every way. We cannot say we are advocates for equality if we write off boys fighting in the playground instead of teaching them other ways to deal with conflict. We cannot claim to be educating children if they leave school not knowing what sexual assault is; what consent is; what harassment is. We cannot argue that we want a more equal future for men and women if we tell our friends to 'man up' when they express emotion. We cannot suggest that we want an end to violence against women if we go online and abuse those we disagree with. We cannot be sincere in our outrage at yet another woman's death if we let jokes about rape float, unchallenged, into our conversations.

A 2021 poll revealed that more than 50 per cent of men said they had changed their behaviour in the aftermath of Sarah Everard's murder: 28 per cent said they would now walk on the opposite side of the road to a woman walking alone; 35 per cent said they were more likely to help a woman who was being harassed.[10] It remains to be seen whether that will lead to long-term changes in male behaviour, or any meaningful difference in women's safety.

In the aftermath of Sarah Everard's murder, thousands of men signed up for a course entitled 'Exploring Masculinities and Allyship Training for Men'. Around 90 per cent did not show up.[11] It might be that the nature of our culture is now that news, movements and ideas are instant, intense and then forgotten. It might be that the real problem remains a lack of desire for meaningful change. If men truly wish to play a part in ending violence against women, their brotherhood needs to be committed and consistent – and it will frequently be uncomfortable. Nobody ever wants to be the person in the room who doesn't laugh when everyone else does. Few people feel comfortable intervening in a situation of escalating violence when doing so might mean they are at risk. But silence is no longer an option. It bears repeating: the culture you get is the behaviour you tolerate. If the endless tidal wave of violence against women is to subside, it requires every man who has ever thought, 'I would never behave that way,' to do something meaningful about it. To change the modern definition of masculinity from one of innate violence to one of moral courage.

There are practical resources available for men who want to be better allies to women but do not know where to start. They range from seminars on rethinking masculinity to advice about bystander intervention and how to be a leader in implementing cultural change. To find out more, see the 'Resources' section at the back of this book.

There are two parts to the conversation about ending violence against women. One centres on how we can change society so that women can safely go where they please and behave as they want without being at risk. The other focuses on how we protect women from the society we currently have, which presents threats of violence, harassment, intimidation and discrimination at every turn. Until we have the former, we cannot stop working on the latter. As things stand, both are vital. It is just as important to protect women in the short term as it is to address male violence for the long term. It is a question of treating the disease itself, and the symptoms of it.

Diversity of ideas is the only way to solve the diversity of problems faced by women. But with that must come a common agreement to prioritise working collectively towards solving the problem. Division is the surest way to frustrate a social movement. As long as those of us seeking change are fighting each other, the powerful can ignore us.

Real change must come at every level. It must come from everyone. It must be sustained. It must be relentless. It must be courageous. It must be resilient. It must translate anger, frustration and despair into action.

It must start now.

It might seem, in the face of the overwhelming unfairness presented on the pages of this book, that change is impossible. Just trying to work out where to begin feels like standing on the edge of an oil spill that stretches to the horizon.

Especially after a lifetime of suffering the effects of misogyny. Especially when the expectation of the emotional labour of women already weighs so heavy. Especially in a society that tells us women should be thankful to have anything at all, that reminds us that women in other countries have it so much worse, that tells women to sit down. Oppression likes its victims alone and grateful. Misogyny likes us quiet.

For those who have suffered directly, silence can be the only way to survive. The right to it is vital. For everyone else, silence is complicity.

I have told you the statistics. Keep them in your phone, in your pocket, in your head. Use them. Demand better.

I have told you the law. Use it. If the law doesn't work, change it. When the law is broken, and if you can, report it. To the police, to your council, to your MP, to your family, to your friends. When the police do not take you seriously, complain. Appeal. Sue. Review. Challenge. Find your sisters. Take them with you. Pick them up. Let them pick you up. Amplify their voices. Organise. Vote. March. Rally. Campaign. Advocate. Interject. Intervene. Refuse to stand by. Refuse to stand down. Remain angry. Stop laughing it off, no matter how much easier and more comfortable that might be. Demand change. Demand it consistently. Demand it now. Accept nothing less than a revolution.

Notes

Introduction

1. Sam Petherick, 'Met officer keeps job after "sharing murder meme" during Sarah Everard search', *Metro* (23 October 2021): https://metro.co.uk/2021/10/23/met-officer-keeps-job-after-sharing-murder-meme-during-sarah-everard-search-15473385/

2. Ellena Cruse, 'Anger after police "tell women not to go out alone" in wake of Sarah Everard's disappearance', MyLondon (10 March 2021): https://www.mylondon.news/news/south-london-news/anger-after-police-tell-women-20047944

3. Joanna Gilmore et al., 'Protesters' experiences of policing at anti-fracking protests in England, 2016–2019', Centre for the Study of Crime, Criminalisation and Social Exclusion/Liverpool John Moores University (2019): https://researchonline.ljmu.ac.uk/id/eprint/11633/1/Gilmore%20Jackson%20Monk%20and%20Short%202019%20National%20Report%20small%207.pdf

4. *R v Sharples* (1989) 12 WLUK 62

5. *R v R* (1991) UKHL 12, British and Irish Legal Information Institute (23 October 1991): https://www.bailii.org/uk/cases/UKHL/1991/12.html
6. Caelainn Barr and Alexandra Topping, 'Fewer than one in 60 rape cases lead to charge in England and Wales', *Guardian* (23 May 2021): https://www.theguardian.com/society/2021/may/23/fewer-than-one-in-60-cases-lead-to-charge-in-england-and-wales

Part One: VIOLENCE AGAINST WOMEN AND GIRLS: THE STATUS QUO

Homicide

1. For 'diminished responsibility' to apply, it has to be established that the abnormality of mental functioning arose from a recognised medical condition, and that it had substantially impaired the killer's ability to understand the nature of what they were doing, to form a rational judgment or to exercise self-control, which provided an explanation for their conduct at the time of the killing.
2. Lizzie Dearden, '93% of killers in England and Wales are men, official figures show', *Independent* (11 March 2021): https://www.independent.co.uk/news/uk/crime/women-murders-men-ons-sarah-everard-b1815779.html
3. 'Homicide in England and Wales: year ending March 2018', Office for National Statistics (7 February 2019): https://www.ons.gov.uk/peoplepopulationandcommunity/crimeandjustice/articles/homicideinenglandandwales/yearendingmarch2018#how-are-victims-and-suspects-related

4. Femicide Census, 'UK Femicides 2009–2018' (2020), p. 15: https://www.femicidecensus.org/wp-content/uploads/2020/11/Femicide-Census-10-year-report.pdf

5. Yvonne Roberts, 'End femicide: 278 dead – the hidden scandal of older women killed by men', *Guardian* (7 March 2021): https://www.theguardian.com/society/2021/mar/07/end-femicide-278-dead-the-hidden-scandal-of-older-women-killed-by-men

6. Femicide Census, 'UK Femicides 2009–2018' (2020), p. 54: https://www.femicidecensus.org/wp-content/uploads/2020/11/Femicide-Census-10-year-report.pdf

7. Ibid., p. 53.

8. 'Homicide in England and Wales: year ending March 2020', Office for National Statistics (25 February 2021), Table 16a: https://www.ons.gov.uk/peoplepopulation andcommunity/crimeandjustice/articles/homicidein englandandwales/yearendingmarch2020

9. Connie Mitchell and Deirdre Anglin, *Intimate Partner Violence: A Health-based Perspective* (Oxford: Oxford University Press, 2009), p. 325. The actual percentage is likely to be significantly higher, as in 23 per cent of cases a lack of information meant it was not possible to establish whether overkilling was present or not; Femicide Census, 'UK Femicides 2009–2018' (2020), p. 41: https://www.femicidecensus.org/wp-content/uploads/2020/11/Femicide-Census-10-year-report.pdf

10. Judge's sentencing remarks: https://www.judiciary.uk/wp-content/uploads/2018/07/r-v-david-clark-sentencing.pdf

11. Richard Vernalls, 'Murder suspect accused of stabbing wife to death because she belittled the size of his penis

claims "lesbian affair" at centre of argument', *Daily Record* (15 June 2018): https://www.dailyrecord.co.uk/news/uk-world-news/murder-suspect-accused-stabbing-wife-12715353

12. Jane Wharton, 'Husband killed his wife after she mocked the size of his penis', *Metro* (28 June 2018): https://metro.co.uk/2018/06/28/husband-killed-wife-mocked-size-penis-7667004/

13. 'Man murdered wife after sending messages to relatives alleging lesbian affair, court hears', *Independent* (19 June 2018): https://www.independent.co.uk/news/uk/crime/david-clark-murder-trial-latest-melanie-lesbian-affair-messages-worcestershire-a8405961.html

14. Mark Cardwell and Kelly-Ann Mills, 'Estate agent "stabbed wife to death in rage" after row about her lesbian affair and taunts over his "small d**k"', *Mirror* (7 June 2018): https://www.mirror.co.uk/news/uk-news/estate-agent-stabbed-wife-death-12663896

15. Martin Fricker and James Rodger, 'First picture of "lover in lesbian tryst row" which saw estate agent kill wife over "small penis" jibes', *Birmingham Mail* (28 June 2018): https://www.birminghammail.co.uk/news/midlands-news/first-picture-lover-lesbian-tryst-14838705

16. Richard Spillett, 'Pictured: The daughter of estate agent's best friend whose tryst with his wife led to murder after she taunted him about his failings as a man', *Daily Mail* (27 June 2018): https://www.dailymail.co.uk/news/article-5890857/Estate-agent-killed-wife-row-lesbian-affair.html

17. Frances Perraudin, 'Femicide in UK: 76% of women killed by men in 2017 knew their killer', *Guardian* (18 December

2018): https://www.theguardian.com/uk-news/2018/
dec/18/femicide-in-uk-76-of-women-killed-by-men-in-2017-
knew-their-killer
18. Femicide Census, 'UK Femicides 2009–2018' (2020),
p. 53: https://www.femicidecensus.org/wp-content/
uploads/2020/11/Femicide-Census-10-year-report.pdf
19. Ibid.

Sexual Violence
1. Joint enterprise is a doctrine of criminal law that allows
two or more people to be convicted of the same crime
regarding the same incident, even if they had different
types or levels of involvement in it. The classic example is
of a bank robbery, where the getaway driver is as guilty of
the robbery as the person threatening the bank clerk,
even though the getaway driver might never set foot in
the bank.
2. Rape Crisis England & Wales: https://rapecrisis.org.uk/
get-informed/about-sexual-violence/statistics-sexual-
violence/
3. 'Sexual offences victim characteristics, England and
Wales: year ending March 2020', Office for National
Statistics (18 March 2021), Table 7: https://www.ons.gov.
uk/peoplepopulationandcommunity/crimeandjustice/
articles/sexualoffencesvictimcharacteristicsengland
andwales/latest
4. Dawn Foster, 'Homeless women are even more
vulnerable than homeless men', *Guardian* (14 February
2017): https://www.theguardian.com/housing-network/
2017/feb/14/homelessness-women-disadvantaged-channel-
4-councils

5. 'Nature of sexual assault by rape or penetration, England and Wales: year ending March 2020', Office for National Statistics (18 March 2021), Table 16: https://www.ons.gov.uk/peoplepopulationandcommunity/crimeandjustice/datasets/natureofsexualassaultbyrapeorpenetrationenglandandwales

6. 'Why do so few rape cases go to court?', BBC News (27 May 2022): bbc.co.uk/news/uk-48095118

7. Caelainn Barr and Alexandra Topping, 'Rape convictions fall to record low in England and Wales', *Guardian* (30 July 2020): https://www.theguardian.com/society/2020/jul/30/convictions-fall-record-low-england-wales-prosecutions

8. 'PR: Rape Prosecutions – Today's Judgment', Centre for Women's Justice (15 March 2021): https://www.centreforwomensjustice.org.uk/news/2021/3/15/pr-rape-prosecutions-todays-judgment; 'The end-to-end rape review report on findings and actions', HM Government (June 2021): https://assets.publishing.service.gov.uk/government/uploads/system/uploads/attachment_data/file/1001417/end-to-end-rape-review-report-with-correction-slip.pdf

9. 'Charging perverting the course of justice and wasting police time in cases involving allegedly false rape and domestic violence allegations', Alison Levitt KC, Principal Legal Advisor, and the Crown Prosecution Service Equality and Diversity Unit (March 2013): https://www.cps.gov.uk/sites/default/files/documents/legal_guidance/perverting-course-of-justice-march-2013.pdf

10. Liz Kelly, Jo Lovett and Linda Regan, 'A gap or a chasm? Attrition in reported rape cases', Home Office Research Study 293 (2005): https://www.researchgate.net/

publication/238713283_Home_Office_Research_Study_293_
A_gap_or_a_chasm_Attrition_in_reported_rape_cases

11. 'Nature of sexual assault by rape or penetration, England and Wales: year ending March 2020', Office for National Statistics (18 March 2021), Table 1: https://www.ons.gov. uk/peoplepopulationandcommunity/crimeandjustice/ datasets/natureofsexualassaultbyrapeorpenetration englandandwales

12. 'Nature of sexual assault by rape or penetration, England and Wales: year ending March 2020', Office for National Statistics (18 March 2021), Table 8: https://www.ons.gov. uk/peoplepopulationandcommunity/crimeandjustice/ datasets/natureofsexualassaultbyrapeorpenetration englandandwales – 37.9 per cent at the woman's home, 25.8 per cent at the offender's home.

13. 'Nature of sexual assault by rape or penetration, England and Wales: year ending March 2020', Office for National Statistics (18 March 2021), Table 3: https://www.ons.gov. uk/peoplepopulationandcommunity/crimeandjustice/ datasets/natureofsexualassaultbyrapeorpenetration englandandwales

14. L Ellison et al., 'Challenging criminal justice? Psychosocial disability and rape victimization', *Criminology and Criminal Justice*, 15: 2 (2015), pp. 225–44.

15. YouGov/End Violence Against Women Coalition Survey Results (19 September 2018): https://www.endviolence againstwomen.org.uk/wp-content/uploads/Data-tables-for-Attitudes-to-Sexual-Consent-research-report.pdf

16. Ibid.

17. Maya Oppenheim, 'Majority of men believe women more likely to be sexually assaulted if wearing revealing clothes,

study suggests', *Independent* (23 February 2019): https://www.independent.co.uk/news/uk/home-news/ men-sexual-assault-clothes-women-victim-blaming-rape-a8792591.html

18. 'National LGBT Survey Summary Report', Government Equalities Office (July 2018): https://assets.publishing. service.gov.uk/government/uploads/system/uploads/ attachment_data/file/722314/GEO-LGBT-Survey-Report.pdf

19. Colleen A Ward, *Attitudes Towards Rape: Feminist and Social Psychological Perspectives* (Sage Publications, 1995).

Domestic Abuse

1. As compared with 757,000 men. 'Domestic abuse in England and Wales overview: November 2020', Office for National Statistics (November 2020): https://www.ons. gov.uk/peoplepopulationandcommunity/crimeandjustice/ bulletins/domesticabuseinenglandandwalesoverview/ november2020

2. Our Work, Refuge: https://www.refuge.org.uk/our-work/ forms-of-violence-and-abuse/domestic-violence/domestic-violence-the-facts/

3. 'Domestic abuse in England and Wales overview: November 2020', Office for National Statistics (November 2020): https://www.ons.gov.uk/peoplepopulationand community/crimeandjustice/bulletins/domesticabuse inenglandandwalesoverview/november2020

4. S Walby and J S Towers, 'Measuring violence to end violence: mainstreaming gender', *Journal of Gender-Based Violence*, 1: 1 (2017), pp. 11-31: https://openaccess.city.ac.

uk/id/eprint/21543/1/Measuring%20violence%20to%20
end%20violence.pdf

5. 'Crime in England and Wales: year ending March 2020',
Office for National Statistics (17 July 2020): https://www.
ons.gov.uk/peoplepopulationandcommunity/crimeand
justice/bulletins/crimeinenglandandwales/yearending
march2020; S Walby and J S Towers (2017); S Walby and J
Allen, 'Domestic violence, sexual assault and stalking:
findings from the British Crime Survey', Home Office
Research Study (2004): https://openaccess.city.ac.uk/id/
eprint/21697/1/Domesticviolencefindings_2004_5British
CrimeSurvey276.pdf

6. Professor Sylvia Walby, 'The cost of domestic violence',
Women and Equality Unit (September 2004): https://
eprints.lancs.ac.uk/id/eprint/55255/1/cost_of_dv_report_
sept04.pdf

7. Ruth Aitken and Vanessa Munro, 'Domestic abuse and
suicide: exploring the links with Refuge's client base and
work force', London: University of Warwick, School of
Law: Refuge (2018): http://wrap.warwick.ac.uk/103609/

8. 'Ahead of Black History Month, Refuge calls for better
protection for Black women experiencing domestic
abuse', Refuge blog (30 September 2021): https://www.
refuge.org.uk/refuge-better-protection-of-black-women-
domestic-abuse/

9. 'Adjournment Debate: Black Women and Domestic Abuse
– 30 June 2020', Joint briefing by Imkaan and the End
Violence Against Women Coalition (June 2020): https://
www.endviolenceagainstwomen.org.uk/wp-content/
uploads/Joint-Briefing-for-Meg-Hillier-MP-Debate-EVAW-
Imkaan.pdf

10. 'Disabled Survivors Too: Disabled people and domestic abuse', SafeLives (March 2017): https://safelives.org.uk/sites/default/files/resources/Disabled%20Survivors%20Too%20CORRECTED.pdf

11. 'LGBT in Britain: Home and Communities', YouGov/Stonewall (2017), p. 9: https://www.stonewall.org.uk/sites/default/files/lgbt_in_britain_home_and_communities.pdf

12. 'Supporting trans women in domestic and sexual violence services', Stonewall/nfpSynergy (2018): https://www.stonewall.org.uk/system/files/stonewall_and_nfpsynergy_report.pdf

13. 'Out of sight, out of mind? Transgender People's Experiences of Domestic Abuse', Scottish Transgender Alliance/Stop Domestic Abuse (August 2010): https://www.scottishtrans.org/wp-content/uploads/2013/03/trans_domestic_abuse.pdf

14. Joanne Bretherton and Nicholas Pearce, 'Women and Rough Sleeping: A Critical Review of Current Research and Methodology', University of York/Centre for Housing Policy (2018): https://www.mungos.org/publication/women-and-rough-sleeping-a-critical-review/

15. 'Domestic abuse in England and Wales overview: November 2020', Office for National Statistics (November 2020): https://www.ons.gov.uk/peoplepopulationand community/crimeandjustice/bulletins/domesticabusein englandandwalesoverview/november2020; Dina Sherif, 'Covid-19 and the Surge in Domestic Abuse in the UK', Centre for Women's Justice (10 November 2020): https://www.centreforwomensjustice.org.uk/new-blog-1/2020/11/10/covid-19-and-surge-in-domestic-abuse-in-uk

16. Maya Oppenheim, '"It's the hardest time of year": why domestic violence spikes over Christmas', *New Statesman* (22 December 2015): https://www.newstatesman.com/politics/2015/12/it-s-hardest-time-year-why-domestic-violence-spikes-over-christmas

17. Ria Ivandic, Tom Kirchmaier and Neus Torres-Blas, 'Football, alcohol and domestic abuse', LSE/Centre for Economic Performance (4 July 2021): https://cep.lse.ac.uk/_NEW/PUBLICATIONS/abstract.asp?index=8216

18. Domestic abuse in pregnancy, NHS: https://www.nhs.uk/pregnancy/support/domestic-abuse-in-pregnancy/

19. Femicide Census, 'UK Femicides 2009–2018' (2020), p. 30: https://www.femicidecensus.org/wp-content/uploads/2020/11/Femicide-Census-10-year-report.pdf

20. Emily Bartholomew, 'Domestic violence charity Sistah Space marks five years since the murders of "community giant" Valerie Forde and her baby daughter', *Hackney Gazette* (21 February 2019): https://www.hackneygazette.co.uk/news/remembering-valerie-forde-and-her-baby-daughter-3620114

21. Joe Roberts, 'Black women scared to report domestic abuse in case Home Office deports them', *Metro* (27 February 2020): https://metro.co.uk/2020/02/27/black-women-scared-report-domestic-abuse-case-home-office-deports-12313855/

22. Our Work, Refuge: refuge.org.uk/our-work/forms-of-violence-and-abuse/domestic-violence/effects-of-domestic-violence-on-women/

Female Genital Mutilation

1. A J Macfarlane and E Dorkenoo, 'Prevalence of Female Genital Mutilation in England and Wales: National and local estimates', City University London/Equality Now (2015): https://openaccess.city.ac.uk/id/eprint/12382/9/FGM%20statistics%20final%20report%2021%2007%2020 15%20released%20text%20corrected%20Jan%202016%20 20%2001%2016.pdf

2. 'Female genital mutilation (FGM): The facts', HM Government/Home Office: https://assets.publishing. service.gov.uk/government/uploads/system/uploads/attachment_data/file/783684/FGM_The_Facts_A6_v4_web.pdf

3. A J Macfarlane and E Dorkenoo, 'Prevalence of Female Genital Mutilation in England and Wales: National and local estimates', City University London/Equality Now (2015): https://openaccess.city.ac.uk/id/eprint/12382/9/FGM%20statistics%20final%20report%2021%2007%2020 15%20released%20text%20corrected%20Jan%202016%20 20%2001%2016.pdf

4. Hannah Summers, 'Urgent action needed to address lack of FGM awareness, say experts', *Guardian* (2 February 2019): https://www.theguardian.com/society/2019/feb/02/urgent-action-needed-address-lack-fgm-awareness

5. Overview: Female genital mutilation (FGM), NHS: https://www.nhs.uk/conditions/female-genital-mutilation-fgm/

6. 'What is FGM?' End FGM European Network: https://www.endfgm.eu/female-genital-mutilation/what-is-fgm/

7. Overview: Female genital mutilation (FGM), NHS: https://www.nhs.uk/conditions/female-genital-mutilation-fgm/

8. Beth Gulliver, 'I was butchered at just six years old. Now I'm trying to stop FGM which made me want to die', MyLondon (2 October 2021): https://www.mylondon. news/news/east-london-news/fgm-survivor-campaigning-against-mutilation-21711287

9. Lizzie Dearden, 'FGM cutters "being flown into UK to mutilate girls to order", survivor warns', *Independent* (1 October 2018): https://www.independent.co.uk/news/uk/ crime/fgm-uk-female-genital-mutilation-countries-girls-children-cutters-flight-survivor-police-a8560306.html

10. Multi-agency statutory guidance on female genital mutilation, HM Government (2020): https://www.gov.uk/ government/publications/multi-agency-statutory-guidance-on-female-genital-mutilation

11. Lizzie Dearden, '"There was blood everywhere": Survivor among hundreds stopped in FGM crackdown at Heathrow Airport', *Independent* (13 January 2018): https://www. independent.co.uk/news/uk/crime/fgm-female-genital-mutilation-police-heathrow-airport-crackdown-operation-limelight-national-centre-barnardos-a8155981.html

12. Alice Ross, 'FGM: police and border officers target travellers to high-risk countries', *Guardian* (6 September 2016): https://www.theguardian.com/society/2016/ sep/06/fgm-police-border-travellers-high-risk-countries-nigeria-heathrow; Amy Abdelshahid, Dr Kate Smith and Khadra Habane, '"Do no harm": Lived Experiences and Impacts of FGM Safeguarding Policies and Procedures, Bristol study', Forward (February 2021): https://www. forwarduk.org.uk/wp-content/uploads/2021/01/ Forward-FGM-Safeguarding-Research-Report-Bristol-Study-2021.pdf

13. National FGM Support Clinics, NHS: https://www.nhs.uk/ conditions/female-genital-mutilation-fgm/national-fgm- support-clinics/
14. Hannah Summers and Rebecca Ratcliffe, 'Mother of three-year-old is first person convicted of FGM in UK', *Guardian* (1 February 2019): https://www.theguardian. com/society/2019/feb/01/fgm-mother-of-three-year-old- first-person-convicted-in-uk

Stalking
1. Stalking Protection Act 2019.
2. 'Stalking victims not protected by police, say campaigners': https://www.bbc.co.uk/news/uk- 63668714
3. Ibid.
4. 'Stalking: findings from the Crime Survey for England and Wales', year ending March 2020 (Table 1), Office for National Statistics (25 November 2020): https://www.ons. gov.uk/peoplepopulationandcommunity/crimeandjustice/ datasets/stalkingfindingsfromthecrimesurveyfor englandandwales
5. Stalking: the Facts, Equation: https://equation.org.uk/ stalking-facts/
6. Ibid.
7. *R (on the application of Sharon Grice) v Her Majesty's Senior Coroner of Brighton and Hove* (2020) EWHC 3581 (Admin), British and Irish Legal Information Institute (24 December 2020): https://www.bailii.org/ew/cases/EWHC/ Admin/2020/3581.html
8. As told to Siana Bangura and published in her piece 'What will it take for black women victims of stalking to

be taken seriously?' on online platform Black Ballad (20 September 2021).

9. 'Internet troll jailed for stalking disabled woman', *North Wales Chronicle* (1 August 2018): https://www.northwaleschronicle.co.uk/news/national/16392224.internet-troll-jailed-stalking-disabled-woman/

10. J Korkodeilou, '"No place to hide": stalking victimisation and its psycho-social effects', University of Salford Manchester (2016): http://usir.salford.ac.uk/id/eprint/40774/1/'No%20Place%20to%20Hide',%20Stalking%20Victimisation

11. Tony Thompson, 'All stalking victims suffer lasting psychological damage, new research finds', *Police Professional* (8 April 2019): https://www.policeprofessional.com/news/all-stalking-victims-suffer-lasting-psychological-damage-new-research-finds/

12. J Korkodeilou, '"No place to hide": stalking victimisation and its psycho-social effects', University of Salford Manchester (2016): http://usir.salford.ac.uk/id/eprint/40774/1/'No%20Place%20to%20Hide',%20Stalking%20Victimisation

Street Harassment

1. 'Prevalence and reporting of sexual harassment in UK public spaces', YouGov/UN Women (March 2021), p. 6: https://www.unwomenuk.org/site/wp-content/uploads/2021/03/APPG-UN-Women_Sexual-Harassment-Report_2021.pdf

2. Ibid p. 17.

3. Ibid p. 18.

4. 'Crime in England and Wales: year ending March 2018', Office for National Statistics (19 July 2018): https://www.ons.gov.uk/peoplepopulationandcommunity/crimeandjustice/bulletins/crimeinenglandandwales/yearendingmarch2018

5. Ibid.

6. 'Trans Lives Survey 2021: Enduring the UK's hostile environment', TransActual (2021): https://static1.squarespace.com/static/5e8a0a6bb02c73725b24dc9d/t/6152eac81e0b0109491dc518/1632824024793/Trans+Lives+Survey+2021.pdf

7. Dr Cerys Bradley, 'Transphobic Hate Crime Report 2020: The scale and impact of transphobic violence, abuse and prejudice', Galop (2020): https://galop.org.uk/wp-content/uploads/2021/06/Trans-Hate-Crime-Report-2020.pdf

8. Joanne Bretherton and Nicholas Pearce, 'Women and Rough Sleeping: A Critical Review of Current Research and Methodology', University of York/Centre for Housing Policy (2018): https://www.mungos.org/publication/women-and-rough-sleeping-a-critical-review/

9. Jemma Crew, 'Disabled woman fears hate crime occurs "more than anyone is ready to admit"', *Evening Standard* (6 October 2021): https://www.standard.co.uk/news/uk/london-home-office-london-school-of-economics-b958989.html

10. Lucy Webster, 'The everyday assault of disabled women: "It's inappropriate sexual touching at least once a month"', *Guardian* (25 November 2021): https://www.theguardian.com/world/2021/nov/25/the-everyday-assault-of-disabled-women-its-

inappropriate-sexual-touching-at-least-once-
a-month

11. Amy Kavanagh and Hannah Mason-Bish, 'As a disabled woman, I'm harassed on the street daily – where's my #MeToo moment?' *Huffington Post* (29 July 2019): https://www.huffingtonpost.co.uk/entry/disabled-woman-me-too_uk_5d3eaee2e4b0db8affaadf12

12. 'How Disabled Women and Non-binary People Experience Non-consensual Touching', Private Places, Public Spaces blog (8 November 2019): https://privateplacespublicspacesblog.wordpress.com/

13. *'I'd Just Like to Be Free': Young Women Speak Out About Sexual Harassment*, Purple Drum/Imkaan/End Violence Against Women Coalition (2016): https://www.youtube.com/watch?v=lJ-qpvibpdU

14. Hannah Mason-Bish and Irene Zempi, 'Misogyny, Racism and Islamophobia: Street Harassment at the Intersections': http://irep.ntu.ac.uk/id/eprint/33475/1/10996_Zempi.pdf

Online Harassment

1. 'Online abuse of women widespread in UK', Amnesty International UK (poll conducted June 2017): https://www.amnesty.org.uk/online-abuse-women-widespread

2. Ibid.

3. Ibid.

4. 'We need more women: Urgent action needed on women's representation', Fawcett Society: https://www.fawcettsociety.org.uk/blog/we-need-more-women-urgent-action-needed-on-womens-representation

5. 'UK: Online abuse against black women MPs "chilling"', Amnesty International (9 June 2020): https://www.amnesty.org.uk/press-releases/uk-online-abuse-against-black-women-mps-chilling

6. 'Revenge porn victims have doubled in last two years, figures suggest', Sky News (25 March 2021): https://news.sky.com/story/revenge-porn-victims-have-doubled-in-last-two-years-figures-suggest-12255933

7. Jessica Ringrose, Kaitlyn Regehr and Betsy Milne, 'Understanding and Combatting Youth Experiences of Image-based Sexual Harassment and Abuse', UCL's Collaborative Social Science Domain/School of Sexuality Education/University of Kent/Association of School and College Leaders (December 2021), p. 29: https://www.ascl.org.uk/ASCL/media/ASCL/Our%20view/Campaigns/Understanding-and-combatting-youth-experiences-of-image-based-sexual-harassment-and-abuse-full-report.pdf

8. Ibid.

9. Ibid.

10. Michael Baggs, 'Online bullying: "I've blocked nearly 10,000 abusive accounts"', BBC News (8 February 2021): https://www.bbc.co.uk/news/newsbeat-55668872

11. 'Black and Asian women MPs abused more online', Amnesty International UK (study conducted 1 January-8 June 2017): https://www.amnesty.org.uk/online-violence-women-mps

12. UK Elections: Abuse and Intimidation, House of Commons debate, Hansard, Vol. 627 (debated on 12 July 2017): https://hansard.parliament.uk/commons/2017-07-12/debates/577970DD-1AEF-4071-8AE0-3E3FC6753C6A/UKElectionsAbuseAndIntimidation

13. Marianna Spring, 'I get abuse and threats online – why can't it be stopped?' BBC News (18 October 2021): https://www.bbc.co.uk/news/uk-58924168

14. Lois Beckett, 'The misogynist incel movement is spreading. Should it be classified as a terror threat?' *Guardian* (3 March 2021): https://www.theguardian.com/lifeandstyle/2021/mar/03/incel-movement-terror-threat-canada

15. Matthew Weaver and Steven Morris, 'Plymouth gunman: a hate-filled misogynist and "incel"', *Guardian* (13 August 2021): https://www.theguardian.com/uk-news/2021/aug/13/plymouth-shooting-suspect-what-we-know-jake-davison

16. Tom Bell, 'Massive rise in use of incel sites that call for women to be raped', *The Times* (3 January 2022): https://www.thetimes.co.uk/article/massive-rise-in-use-of-incel-sites-that-call-for-women-to-be-raped-hddbq5mgc

A Culture of Violence and its Impact on Women

1. 'Perceptions of personal safety and experiences of harassment, Great Britain', Office for National Statistics (June 2021): https://www.ons.gov.uk/peoplepopulationandcommunity/crimeandjustice/datasets/perceptionsofpersonalsafetyandexperiencesofharassmentgreatbritain

2. Ibid.

3. Ibid.

4. Ibid.

5. 'Street Harassment: It's Not OK', Plan International UK (2018): https://plan-uk.org/file/plan-uk-street-harassment-reportpdf/download?token=CyKwYGSJ

Part Two: A JUSTICE SYSTEM THAT FAILS WOMEN

Fair Trials

1. 'Safety in Custody Statistics, England and Wales: Deaths in Prison Custody to September 2021, Assaults and Self-harm to June 2021', Her Majesty's Prison and Probation Service/Ministry of Justice (28 October 2021): https://www.gov.uk/government/statistics/safety-in-custody-quarterly-update-to-june-2021/safety-in-custody-statistics-england-and-wales-deaths-in-prison-custody-to-september-2021-assaults-and-self-harm-to-june-2021

2. 'Prisons can seriously damage your mental health', Prison Reform Trust (2017): http://www.prisonreformtrust.org.uk/uploads/documents/Mentalhealthsmall.pdf

Policing Women

1. Maggie Oliver, 'The real angel of the north: The abuse of young girls by Rochdale sex gangs is one of the great scandals of our time. In a shattering new book, the policewoman who revealed the truth breaks her silence – and shames the superiors who betrayed her ...' *Daily Mail* (10 July 2019): https://www.dailymail.co.uk/femail/article-7234013/Policewoman-revealed-truth-Rochdale-sex-gangs-breaks-silence.html

2. Charlotte Bateman, 'Sexual violence allegations brought by disabled women "not going to court", campaign group says', Sky News (1 August 2021): https://news.sky.com/story/sexual-violence-allegations-brought-by-disabled-women-not-going-to-court-charity-says-12368315

3. In some less serious cases, the police can make the decision to prosecute without needing to refer a case to the CPS.

4. 'Sexual offending: victimisation and the path through the criminal justice system', Office for National Statistics (December 2018): https://www.ons.gov.uk/people populationandcommunity/crimeandjustice/articles/ sexualoffendingvictimisationandthepaththroughthe criminaljusticesystem/2018-12-13

5. William Blackstone, *Commentaries on the Law of England* (Clarendon, 1765).

6. 'The Crown Court Compendium', Judicial College (August 2021), pp. 20-1: https://www.judiciary.uk/wp-content/ uploads/2021/08/Crown-Court-Compendium-Part-I.pdf

7. Caelainn Barr and Alexandra Topping, 'Fewer than one in 60 rape cases lead to charge in England and Wales', *Guardian* (23 May 2021): https://www.theguardian.com/ society/2021/may/23/fewer-than-one-in-60-cases-lead-to- charge-in-england-and-wales

8. 'Annex: Statistics on the number of police officers assaulted in the year ending March 2021, England and Wales', HM Government/Home Office (28 July 2021): https://www.gov.uk/government/statistics/police- workforce-england-and-wales-31-march-2021/ annex-statistics-on-the-number-of-police-officers- assaulted-in-the-year-ending-march-2021-england-and- wales

9. Police Performance Tracker 2019, Institute for Government: https://www.instituteforgovernment.org.uk/ publication/performance-tracker-2019/police; Rachel Schraer, 'Have police numbers dropped?' BBC News (26

July2019): https://www.bbc.co.uk/news/uk-47225797; 'Number of police recorded crime offences in England and Wales from 2002/03 to 2020/21', Statista (10 January 2022): https://www.statista.com/statistics/283069/crimes-in-england-and-wales/

10. Haroon Siddique, 'Two-fifths of police forces in England and Wales lack rape units', *Guardian* (10 October 2021): https://www.theguardian.com/society/2021/oct/10/two-fifths-police-forces-england-and-wales-lack-specialist-rape-units

11. Ibid.

12. Lizzie Dearden, 'Boris Johnson's promise of 20,000 officers isn't enough to solve crime problems, says Britain's most senior police chief', *Independent* (4 January 2020): https://www.independent.co.uk/news/uk/home-news/boris-johnson-police-officers-cuts-austerity-tory-crime-martin-hewitt-a9269481.html

13. Hannah Devlin, 'Police outsource digital forensic work to unaccredited labs', *Guardian* (12 February 2018): https://www.theguardian.com/uk-news/2018/feb/12/police-outsource-digital-forensic-work-to-unaccredited-labs

14. Ibid.

15. Lizzie Dearden, 'Police urge government to scrap plans for "damaging" force league tables', *Independent* (22 April 2021): https://www.independent.co.uk/news/uk/home-news/police-league-tables-targets-crime-b1835911.html

16. Joe Middleton, 'Met Police issues advice to women to "shout or wave a bus down" if they don't trust a male officer', *Independent* (1 October 2021): https://www.independent.co.uk/news/uk/home-news/met-police-sarah-everard-couzens-b1930331.html

17. Jane Merrick, 'Calling Wayne Couzens a "former" police officer lets the Met off the hook for failing Sarah Everard', *i* (30 September 2021): https://inews.co.uk/opinion/wayne-couzens-sarah-everard-killer-former-police-officer-let-met-off-hook-1225799

18. 'At least 16 serving or former police officers have killed women. Why does this matter?' Femicide Census: https://www.femicidecensus.org/at-least-16-serving-or-former-police-officers-have-killed-women-why-does-this-matter/

19. Lucy Campbell, 'West Midlands police officer convicted of assaulting woman resigns', *Guardian* (23 March 2021): https://www.theguardian.com/uk-news/2021/mar/23/west-midlands-police-officer-convicted-of-assaulting-woman-resigns

20. Josh Bolton, 'Met Police officer sacked after strangling his partner and forcing her to lie about her injuries', MyLondon (5 January 2022): https://www.mylondon.news/news/south-london-news/met-police-officer-sacked-after-22576179

21. Christian Fuller, 'Police officer Neil Corbel may have used anti-terror skills to film naked woman in Brighton, court told', *The Argus* (3 November 2021): https://www.theargus.co.uk/news/19690431.police-officer-neil-corbel-may-used-anti-terror-skills-film-naked-women-brighton-court-told/

22. Jem Bartholomew, 'Met detective jailed for three years after spying on naked woman', *Guardian* (21 January 2022): https://www.theguardian.com/uk-news/2022/jan/21/met-detective-jailed-for-three-years-after-spying-on-naked-women

23. A suspended sentence is a custodial sentence where the offender does not have to go to prison on the condition that they commit no further offences during the active period (up to two years) and comply with any requirements imposed, such as unpaid work or a curfew order. Lewis Berrill, 'Met Police officer sentenced for child porn', *Enfield Independent* (26 May 2021): https://www.enfieldindependent.co.uk/news/19329705.met-police-officer-sentenced-child-porn/

24. 'Met Police officer guilty of spying on woman in shower with iPhone', ITV News (10 June 2021): https://www.itv.com/news/london/2021-06-10/met-police-officer-guilty-of-spying-on-woman-in-shower-at-london-flat?fbclid=IwAR1V8xkhfGuGN_wBZiYLB1eugMPIbbXpdZ8FoZTBSe6faCvtJplf-T2jFfk

25. 'Derek Seekings: Police sergeant jailed for rape during break', BBC News (13 January 2021): https://www.bbc.co.uk/news/uk-england-55649934

26. Vikram Dodd, 'Two Met police officers jailed over photos of murdered sisters', *Guardian* (6 December 2021): https://www.theguardian.com/uk-news/2021/dec/06/two-met-police-officers-jailed-photos-murdered-sisters-deniz-jaffer-jamie-lewis-nicole-smallman-bibaa-henry

27. James Bayley, '"Manipulative" police officer, 64, who had sexual relationship with one woman he was assigned to help and groped another is jailed for 18 months', *Daily Mail* (4 October 2021): https://www.dailymail.co.uk/news/article-10058363/Police-officer-64-sexual-relationship-woman-assigned-help-jailed.html

28. As reported on *Dispatches*: 'Cops on Trial', Channel 4 (11 October 2021): https://www.channel4.com/programmes/cops-on-trial-dispatches/on-demand/72730-001
29. 'Retired police officer's misconduct sentence doubled following referral', Attorney General's Office, Gov.uk (30 November 2021): https://www.gov.uk/government/news/retired-police-officers-misconduct-sentence-doubled-following-referral
30. Jon Sharman, '2,000 police officers accused of sexual misconduct in past four years', *Independent* (11 October 2021): https://www.independent.co.uk/news/uk/home-news/police-sexual-misconduct-uk-b1935993.html
31. Ibid.
32. 'Operation Hotton Learning Report', Independent Office for Police Conduct (January 2022): https://www.policeconduct.gov.uk/sites/default/files/Operation%20Hotton%20Learning%20report%20-%20January%202022.pdf
33. As reported on *Dispatches*: 'Cops on Trial', Channel 4 (11 October 2021): https://www.channel4.com/programmes/cops-on-trial-dispatches/on-demand/72730-001
34. Sascha Lavin, 'More than half of Met police officers found guilty of sexual misconduct kept their jobs', *Byline Times* (20 September 2021): https://bylinetimes.com/2021/09/20/more-than-half-of-met-police-officers-found-guilty-of-sexual-misconduct-kept-their-jobs/
35. Casey report, page 11: https://www.met.police.uk/SysSiteAssets/media/downloads/met/about-us/baroness-casey-review/baroness-casey-review-interim-report-on-misconduct.pdf

36. Interim Report of Baroness Casey, page 7: https://www.
met.police.uk/SysSiteAssets/media/downloads/met/
about-us/baroness-casey-review/baroness-casey-review-
interim-report-on-misconduct.pdf

37. The super-complaints system allows designated
organisations to raise issues on behalf of the public about
harmful patterns or trends in policing. 'Police officers
allowed to abuse with impunity in the "locker-room
culture" in UK forces, super-complaint reveals', Centre
for Women's Justice (9 March 2020): https://www.
centreforwomensjustice.org.uk/news/2020/3/9/police-
officers-allowed-to-abuse-with-impunity-in-the-locker-
room-culture-of-uk-forces-super-complaint-reveals;
Centre for Women's Justice super-complaint: https://
static1.squarespace.com/static/5aa98420f2e6b1ba
0c874e42/t/5e690390c104fd669e8c1bbe/1583940498025/
super-complaint2+report.FINAL.2.pdf

38. Centre for Women's Justice super-complaint, p. 13:
https://static1.squarespace.com/static/5aa98420f2e
6b1ba0c874e42/t/5e690390c104fd669e8c1bbe/
1583940498025/super-complaint2+report.FINAL.2.pdf

39. Ibid., pp. 11–26.

40. https://assets.publishing.service.gov.uk/government/
uploads/system/uploads/attachment_data/file/1086988/
police-perpetrated-domestic-abuse-report-cwj-super-
complaint.pdf

41. Beth Mann, 'More Britons now unconfident than
confident in the police to deal with crime locally', YouGov
(6 October 2021): https://yougov.co.uk/topics/politics/
articles-reports/2021/10/06/more-britons-now-
unconfident-confident-police-deal

42. YouGov/End Violence Against Women Coalition Survey Results (2021): https://www.endviolenceagainstwomen. org.uk/wp-content/uploads/EVAW_SexualViolence_ 211028-1.xls-Compatibility-Mode.pdf

Women in Court

1. Caelainn Barr, Owen Bowcott, Alexandra Topping, 'CPS secretly dropped "weak" rape cases, say rights groups', *Guardian* (30 June 2020): https://www.theguardian.com/ law/2020/jun/30/cps-secretly-dropped-weak-cases-say-rights-groups
2. Ibid.
3. 'The end-to-end rape review report on findings and actions', HM Government (June 2021), p. i: https://assets. publishing.service.gov.uk/government/uploads/system/ uploads/attachment_data/file/1001417/end-to-end-rape-review-report-with-correction-slip.pdf
4. Caelainn Barr and Alexandra Topping, 'CPS accused of betraying rape victims as prosecutions hit record low', *Guardian* (22 July 2021): https://www.theguardian.com/ law/2021/jul/22/cps-accused-of-betraying-victims-as-prosecutions-hit-record-low
5. Ibid.
6. Ibid.
7. Rachel George (Home Office) and Sophie Ferguson (Ministry of Justice), 'Review into the Criminal Justice System response to adult rape and serious sexual offences across England and Wales: Research Report' (June 2021), p. 46: https://assets.publishing.service.gov.uk/ government/uploads/system/uploads/attachment_data/ file/994817/rape-review-research-report.pdf

ENOUGH

8. Ibid.
9. Ibid.
10. Georgina Sturge and Sally Lipscombe, 'Is the criminal justice system fit for purpose?' House of Commons Library (15 January 2020): https://commonslibrary. parliament.uk/is-the-criminal-justice-system-fit-for-purpose/
11 'Disclosure of evidence in criminal cases: Eleventh report of session 2017-19', House of Commons Justice Committee (20 July 2018): https://publications. parliament.uk/pa/cm201719/cmselect/cmjust/859/859. pdf#page=20
12. 'FDA response to Boris Johnson's £85m CPS cash injection', FDA (12 August 2019): https://www.fda.org.uk/ home/Newsandmedia/Pressreleases/fda-response-boris-johnson-cps-cash-injection-funding.aspx
13. Patrick Worrall, 'FactCheck: extra funding for CPS comes after long-term cuts', 4 News (23 June 2021): https://www. channel4.com/news/factcheck/factcheck-extra-funding-for-cps-comes-after-long-term-cuts
14. The latest available figures showed that in 2018 around 7.7 per cent of defendants were unrepresented at their first hearing, with 1 per cent unrepresented for their trial. 'The number of litigants in person in crown court rising sharply', Magistrates Association (18 November 2019): https://www.magistrates-association.org.uk/News-and-Comments/the-number-of-litigants-in-person-in-crown-court-rising-sharply
15. Domestic Abuse Act 2021: https://www.legislation.gov.uk/ ukpga/2021/17/part/5/crossheading/prohibition-of-crossexamination-in-person/enacted

178

16. Youth Justice and Criminal Evidence Act 1999, Section 17.

17. 'Advocacy and the Vulnerable (Crime)', The Inns of Court College of Advocacy: https://www.icca.ac.uk/advocacy-the-vulnerable-crime/

18. Frances Gibb, 'The days of brutal trials are at an end', *The Times* (11 May 2017): https://www.thetimes.co.uk/article/the-days-of-brutal-trials-are-at-an-end-stqvwb2z7

19. Dr Jane Monckton, 'Non-fatal Strangulation: A summary report on data collected from SUTDA survey', Stand Up to Domestic Abuse (June 2020): https://sutda.org/wp-content/uploads/Non-fatal-strangulation-Survey-June-2020-.pdf

20. 'PR: Non-fatal Strangulation to Become Stand-alone Offence', Centre for Women's Justice (1 March 2021): https://www.centreforwomensjustice.org.uk/news/2021/3/1/pr-non-fatal-strangulation-to-become-stand-alone-offence

21. Ibid.

22. We Can't Consent to This: https://wecantconsenttothis.uk/aboutus

23. Ibid.

24. Comptroller and Auditor General, 'Reducing the backlog in criminal courts', Session 2021–22, HC 732, National Audit Office (22 October 2021), p. 16: https://www.nao.org.uk/wp-content/uploads/2021/10/Reducing-the-backlog-in-criminal-courts.pdf

25. Haroon Siddique, 'Almost 75,000 defendants awaiting crown court trial, says head of CPS', *Guardian* (1 November 2022): https://www.theguardian.com/law/2022/nov/01/almost-75000-crown-court-cases-backlog-cps-max-hill

26. Flora Thompson, 'Rape victims "lucky" if their case gets to court within four years, MPs told', *Independent* (1 December 2021): https://www.independent.co.uk/news/uk/rape-victims-mps-criminal-bar-association-england-wales-b1967696.html

27. Phil Shepka and Ben Schofield, 'Court backlog: "I don't believe my abuse case will get to court"', BBC News (16 December 2021): https://www.bbc.co.uk/news/uk-england-beds-bucks-herts-59464418

28. Comptroller and Auditor General, 'Reducing the backlog in criminal courts', Session 2021–22, HC 732, National Audit Office (22 October 2021), p. 7: https://www.nao.org.uk/wp-content/uploads/2021/10/Reducing-the-backlog-in-criminal-courts.pdf

29. Section 14 of the Crown Court Manual: https://www.judiciary.uk/wp-content/uploads/JCO/Documents/Protocols/listing_crown_court_manual_050705.pdf

30. 'VC analysis of victims' reasons for withdrawing sexual offence complaints', Victims' Commissioner (15 August 2019): https://s3-eu-west-2.amazonaws.com/victcomm2-prod-storage-119w3o4kq2z48/uploads/2019/08/OVC-analysis-victims-complaints-withdrawal.pdf

31. 'Only 2% of Britain's civil and criminal courthouses are fully accessible', Bolt Burdon Kemp: www.boltburdonkemp.co.uk/campaigns/only-2-percent-british-courthouses-fully-accessible/

32. Heather Saul, 'Lawyer accused child grooming victims of claiming abuse "because it is better to be a victim than a slag"', *Independent* (7 March 2015): https://www.independent.co.uk/news/uk/crime/lawyer-accused-child-

grooming-victims-of-claiming-abuse-because-it-is-better-
to-be-a-victim-than-a-slag-10093066.html

33. *Howard Godfrey v Bar Standards Board* (2018), EWHC
   1409 (Admin): https://static1.squarespace.com/
   static/5c9b72ea0490796e32459415/t/5d07b0e4ca83a500
   0149ede9/1560785128929/Godfrey-v-BSB.pdf

34. Sam Adams, 'David Osborne: Wearing "flimsy dresses"
   suggests girls are "LOOSE and free" claims barrister
   behind sexual consent row', *Mirror* (11 February 2015):
   https://www.mirror.co.uk/news/uk-news/david-osborne-
   wearing-flimsy-dresses-5146443

35. Andy Dolan, 'Fury at the senior barrister who said that if a
   woman is drunk it can't be rape: Victims' groups condemn
   remarks as "simply wrong"', *Daily Mail* (8 February 2015):
   https://www.dailymail.co.uk/news/article-2945192/Fury-
   senior-barrister-said-woman-drunk-t-rape-Victims-groups-
   condemn-remarks-simply-wrong.html

36. He should not be confused with David Peter Osborne,
   also a barrister, who has an unblemished reputation.

37. Fiona Leverick, 'What do we know about rape myths and
   juror decision making?' *The International Journal of
   Evidence & Proof*, 24: 3 (2020), pp. 255–79: https://
   journals.sagepub.com/doi/pdf/10.1177/1365712720923157

38. Ibid.

39. 'Prevalence and reporting of sexual harassment in UK
   public spaces', YouGov/UN Women (March 2021): https://
   www.unwomenuk.org/site/wp-content/uploads/2021/03/
   APPG-UN-Women_Sexual-Harassment-Report_2021.pdf

40. The Facts, Refuge: https://www.refuge.org.uk/our-work/
   forms-of-violence-and-abuse/domestic-violence/domestic-
   violence-the-facts/

41. Press Association, 'Police probe after online troll who stalked disabled women freed from jail early', *In Cumbria* (9 February 2019): https://www.in-cumbria.com/news/17420761.police-probe-online-troll-stalked-disabled-woman-freed-jail-early/

42. 'Why focus on reducing women's imprisonment?' Prison Reform Trust (February 2017): http://www.prisonreformtrust.org.uk/Portals/0/Documents/Women/whywomen.pdf

Part Three: HOW TO END IT

Political Will

1. Domestic Abuse Bill, House of Commons debate, Hansard, Vol. 692 (debated on 15 April 2021): https://hansard.parliament.uk/commons/2021-04-15/debates/0E322BD7-571C-4DC5-A8C8-7B29806DE067/DomesticAbuseBill

2. Police, Crime, Sentencing and Courts Bill, House of Lords debate, Hansard, Vol. 817 (debated on 10 January 2022): https://hansard.parliament.uk/lords/2022-01-10/debates/DE31B0AB-B2E4-4687-B021-6D127741D254/Debate

3. Crime and Disorder Act 1998 and Section 66 of the Sentencing Act 2020.

4. Lizzie Dearden, 'Police leaders back making misogyny a hate crime after Boris Johnson rejects mounting calls', *Independent* (18 November 2021): https://www.independent.co.uk/news/uk/home-news/misogyny-hate-crime-police-everard-b1960325.html

5. Rob Merrick, 'Boris Johnson rules out making misogyny a hate crime because it would overload the police',

Independent (5 October 2021): https://www.independent.
co.uk/news/uk/politics/boris-johnson-women-violence-
police-crime-b1932431.html

6. Police, Crime, Sentencing and Courts Bill, House of Lords
debate, Hansard, Vol. 817 (debated 17 January 2022):
https://hansard.parliament.uk/Lords/2022-01-17/debates/
D4DCBA9B-3C6A-4F1C-B932-5E04908DF13C/
PoliceCrimeSentencingAndCourtsBill

7. 'Misogyny' definition, Dictionary.com: https://www.
dictionary.com/browse/misogyny

8. 'Misandry' definition, Dictionary.com: https://www.
dictionary.com/browse/misandry

9. Feminism entry, Britannica.com: https://www.britannica.
com/topic/feminism

10. 'Dominic Raab corrected over definition of misogyny',
BBC News (6 October 2021): https://www.bbc.co.uk/news/
av/uk-politics-58816108

11. 'Raab on Boris, Brexit, feminism and gender/ITV News',
ITV News YouTube channel (29 May 2019): https://www.
youtube.com/watch?v=FriiFMfRYNQ

12. Rowena Mason, 'Dominic Raab defends calling
feminists "obnoxious bigots"', *Guardian* (26 May 2019):
https://www.theguardian.com/politics/2019/may/
26/dominic-raab-defends-calling-feminists-obnoxious-
bigots

13. https://assets.publishing.service.gov.uk/government/
uploads/system/uploads/attachment_data/file/1074113/
Lobby_Pack_10_May_2022.pdf

14. 'Hate crime laws: Final report', HC 942, Law Commission
(6 December 2021), paragraph 5.392 onwards: https://
s3-eu-west-2.amazonaws.com/lawcom-prod-storage-

11jsxou24uy7q/uploads/2021/12/Hate-crime-report-
accessible.pdf

15. Ibid., paragraph 5.393.

16. 'Ending Public Sexual Harassment: The Case for
    Legislation', Plan International/Our Streets Now
    (November 2020): https://plan-uk.org/file/ending-public-
    sexual-harassment-the-case-for-legislationpdf/
    download?token=YINyyOfW; 72 per cent of girls and 86
    per cent of parents said knowing public sexual
    harassment was a criminal offence would make them
    more likely to report it to the police.

How to Make the Police Safe for Women

1. Police Performance Tracker 2019, Institute for
   Government: https://www.instituteforgovernment.org.uk/
   publication/performance-tracker-2019/police

2. Ibid.

3. Alison Pratt, 'Police stations: Are they a thing of the past?'
   House of Commons Library (28 May 2019):
   commonslibrary.parliament.uk/home-affairs/
   communities/police-stations-are-they-a-thing-of-the-past

4. Haroon Siddique, 'Two-fifths of police forces in England
   and Wales lack rape units', *Guardian* (10 October 2021):
   https://www.theguardian.com/society/2021/oct/10/
   two-fifths-police-forces-england-and-wales-lack-specialist-
   rape-units

5. Comptroller and Auditor General, 'Tackling Serious and
   Organised Crime', Session 2017–2019, HC 2219, National
   Audit Office (28 June 2019), p. 9: https://www.nao.org.uk/
   wp-content/uploads/2019/03/Tackling-serious-and-
   organised-crime.pdf

6. Comptroller and Auditor General, 'Financial Sustainability of Police Forces in England and Wales 2018', Session 2017–2019, HC 1501, National Audit Office (11 September 2018), p. 27: https://www.nao.org.uk/wp-content/uploads/2018/09/Financial-sustainability-of-police-forces-in-England-and-Wales-2018.pdf

7. Gavin Fischer, 'Police officers taken off beat to deal with mental health calls', BBC News (2 September 2019): https://www.bbc.co.uk/news/uk-wales-49498208

8. 'Policing and Mental Health: Picking Up the Pieces', Her Majesty's Inspectorate of Constabulary and Fire & Rescue Services, (November 2018): https://www.justiceinspectorates.gov.uk/hmicfrs/wp-content/uploads/policing-and-mental-health-picking-up-the-pieces.pdf

9. Rachel George (Home Office) and Sophie Ferguson (Ministry of Justice), 'Review into the Criminal Justice System response to adult rape and serious sexual offences across England and Wales: Research Report' (June 2021), p. 85: https://assets.publishing.service.gov.uk/government/uploads/system/uploads/attachment_data/file/994817/rape-review-research-report.pdf

10. Holly Johnson et al., 'Intimate Femicide: The Role of Coercive Control', *Feminist Criminology*, 14: 1 (2019), pp. 3–23: https://journals.sagepub.com/doi/pdf/10.1177/1557085117701574

11. Amy Beecham, 'Sistah Space: domestic abuse charity launch "Valerie's Law" petition and video campaign backed by Michaela Coel and FKA Twigs', *Stylist* (2021): https://www.stylist.co.uk/news/sistah-space-campaign-valeries-law-michaela-coel/566241

12. VALERIE'S LAW: Compulsory Training for Agencies Supporting Black DV Victims, Petition, UK Government and Parliament: https://petition.parliament.uk/petitions/578416

13. Charlotte Bateman, 'Sexual violence allegations brought by disabled women "not going to court", campaign group says', Sky News (1 August 2021): https://news.sky.com/story/sexual-violence-allegations-brought-by-disabled-women-not-going-to-court-charity-says-12368315

14. 'I'm going to sort it' (17 October 2022): https://www.lbc.co.uk/radio/presenters/nick-ferrari/met-chief-evidence-shows-officers-force-treating-women-appallingly/

15. James Gant, 'Ex police chief claims it has taken "death of a white woman" for trust in policing to be addressed after Sarah Everard death as she slams Cressida Dick for Met's lack of action in tackling misogyny', *Daily Mail* (2 October 2021): https://www.dailymail.co.uk/news/article-10051791/Ex-police-chief-slams-Cressida-Dick-lack-action-tackling-misogyny.html

16. 'Sarah Everard: Female officers "fear reporting male colleagues"', BBC News (30 September 2021): https://www.bbc.co.uk/news/uk-58754182

17. Jack Wright, 'Retired female Met detective claims she told Cressida Dick about "vulgar and sexist" WhatsApp messages sent by male officers – but got no response', *Daily Mail* (3 October 2021): https://www.dailymail.co.uk/news/article-10054141/Retired-Met-detective-told-Cressida-Dick-sexist-WhatsApp-messages-sent-male-officers.html; Adela Whittingham, 'Ex detective's warning of "vulgar and sexist" WhatsApp group ignored by Met Police bosses', *Mirror* (2 October 2021): https://www.

mirror.co.uk/news/uk-news/ex-detectives-warning-vulgar-sexist-25125054

18. Aamna Mohdin, 'Senior female officer wants "zero tolerance" on sexist police banter' *Guardian* (2 October 2021); https://www.theguardian.com/uk-news/2021/oct/02/senior-female-officer-wants-zero-tolerance-on-sexist-police-banter

19. 'Police officers allowed to abuse with impunity in the "locker-room culture" in UK forces, super-complaint reveals', Centre for Women's Justice (9 March 2020): https://www.centreforwomensjustice.org.uk/news/2020/3/9/police-officers-allowed-to-abuse-with-impunity-in-the-locker-room-culture-of-uk-forces-super-complaint-reveals

20. Sascha Lavin, 'More than half of Met police officers found guilty of sexual misconduct kept their jobs', *Byline Times* (20 September 2021): https://bylinetimes.com/2021/09/20/more-than-half-of-met-police-officers-found-guilty-of-sexual-misconduct-kept-their-jobs/

21. Super-complaint by Centre for Women's Justice: Failure to address police perpetrated domestic abuse (9 March 2020): https://assets.publishing.service.gov.uk/government/uploads/system/uploads/attachment_data/file/913084/Police_perpetrated_domestic_abuse.pdf

22. Alice Wright, 'Met's "flag down a bus" advice to women wins PM's backing', *Daily Mail* (3 October 2021): https://www.mailplus.co.uk/edition/news/politics/111646/mets-flag-down-a-bus-advice-to-women-wins-pms-backing

A System of Justice

1. Caelainn Barr, Owen Bowcott, Alexandra Topping, 'CPS secretly dropped "weak" rape cases, say rights groups', *Guardian* (30 June 2020): https://www.theguardian.com/law/2020/jun/30/cps-secretly-dropped-weak-cases-say-rights-groups

2. National Statistics, 'Police Workforce, England and Wales: 31 March 2021', HM Government/Home Office (28 July 2021): https://www.gov.uk/government/statistics/police-workforce-england-and-wales-31-march-2021/police-workforce-england-and-wales-31-march-2021; HHJ Emma Nott, 'Gender at the Bar and fair access to work', *Counsel* (4 January 2021): https://www.counselmagazine.co.uk/articles/gender-at-the-bar-fair-access-to-work-(4); Judicial Diversity Statistics 2019 (11 July 2019): https://www.judiciary.uk/wp-content/uploads/2019/07/Judicial-Diversity-Statistics-2019-1-2.pdf

3. Ethnicity facts and figures: Police workforce, HM Government (29 January 2021): https://www.ethnicity-facts-figures.service.gov.uk/workforce-and-business/workforce-diversity/police-workforce/latest#:~:text=White%20people%20made%20up%2092.7,2.2%25%20of%20the%20general%20population; Workforce diversity data, The Crown Prosecution Service: https://www.cps.gov.uk/publication/workforce-diversity-data; Judicial Diversity Statistics 2019 (11 July 2019): https://www.judiciary.uk/wp-content/uploads/2019/07/Judicial-Diversity-Statistics-2019-1-2.pdf

4. Age range and disabled police officers by region in England and Wales, HM Government/Home Office (31 March 2014): https://assets.publishing.service.gov.uk/

government/uploads/system/uploads/attachment_data/
file/375086/Age_range_and_disabled_police_officers_by_
region_in_England_and_Wales_as_at_31_March_2014.pdf;
Workforce diversity data, The Crown Prosecution
Service: https://www.cps.gov.uk/publication/workforce-
diversity-data

5. The Code of Practice for Victims of Crime in England and
Wales, HM Government/Ministry of Justice (last updated
21 April 2021): https://www.gov.uk/government/
publications/the-code-of-practice-for-victims-of-crime

Cultural Change: The Disease and the Symptom

1. 'Domestic abuse prevalence and trends, England and
Wales: year ending March 2020', Office for National
Statistics (25 November 2020): https://www.ons.gov.uk/
peoplepopulationandcommunity/crimeandjustice/
articles/domesticabuseprevalenceandt
rendsenglandandwales/yearendingmarch2020#data-
sources-and-quality

2. Femicide Census, 'UK Femicides 2009-2018' (2020),
p. 53: https://www.femicidecensus.org/wp-content/
uploads/2020/11/Femicide-Census-10-year-report.pdf

3. Herb Weisbaum, 'Big Data knows you're pregnant (and
that's not all)', CNBC (9 April 2014): https://www.cnbc.
com/2014/04/09/big-data-knows-youre-pregnant-and-
thats-not-all.html

4. National FGM Support Clinics, NHS: https://www.nhs.uk/
conditions/female-genital-mutilation-fgm/national-fgm-
support-clinics/

5. 'Barriers Faced by Lesbian, Gay, Bisexual and
Transgender People in Accessing Domestic Abuse,

Stalking and Harassment, and Sexual Violence Services',
Welsh Government Social Research (2014): https://gov.
wales/sites/default/files/statistics-and-research/2019-
07/140604-barriers-faced-lgbt-accessing-domestic-abuse-
services-en.pdf

6. 'Adjournment Debate: Black Women and Domestic Abuse
– 30 June 2020', Joint briefing by Imkaan and the End
Violence Against Women Coalition (June 2020): https://
www.endviolenceagainstwomen.org.uk/wp-content/
uploads/Joint-Briefing-for-Meg-Hillier-MP-Debate-EVAW-
Imkaan.pdf

7. 'Future Men 2018 Survey', YouGov/Working With Men
(November 2018): https://futuremen.org/future-men-2018-
survey/

8. Patrick Butler and agency, 'Male suicide rate hits
two-decade high in England and Wales', *Guardian* (1
September 2020): https://www.theguardian.com/
society/2020/sep/01/male-suicide-rate-england-wales-
covid-19

9. 'How many violent attacks and sexual assaults on women
are there?' BBC News (24 September 2021): https://www.
bbc.co.uk/news/explainers-56365412

10. Julian Druker, Twitter: https://twitter.com/Julian5News/
status/1465710295993618432

11. Gina Martin, Twitter: https://twitter.com/ginamartinuk/
status/1481990374205923329?s=20

Resources

The following is a non-exhaustive list of organisations that can provide support to those who might be affected by the subjects discussed in this book.

Many would also benefit from the financial support of any readers who wish to help them to keep doing their vital work. I urge you to do so if you can.

Beyond Equality

A charity that works to engage men in preventing gender-based violence.

Website: beyondequality.org

Centre for Women's Justice

National charity working with specialist lawyers, academics, activists, survivors and frontline service providers to ensure access to justice for victims of male violence.

Website: centreforwomensjustice.org.uk
Call: 0207 092 1807

Coram Children's Legal Centre

Promotes and protects the rights of children in the UK and internationally.

Website: childrenslegalcentre.com

End Violence Against Women

A leading coalition of specialist women's support services, researchers, activists, survivors and NGOs working to end violence against women and girls.

Website: endviolenceagainstwomen.org.uk
Call: 0203 735 8219

FGM National Clinical Group

A UK-based charity that works with women who have been affected by FGM and other related problems.

Website: fgmnationalgroup.org
Call: 07791 462 415

Galop

Supports LGBT+ people who have experienced abuse and violence.

Website: galop.org.uk
National LGBT+ Domestic Abuse helpline: 0800 999 5428
LGBT+ Hate Crime Helpline: 0207 704 2040
National Conversion Therapy Helpline: 0800 130 3335

Glitch

A UK charity that works to end online abuse, including providing resources on 'being an active bystander'.

Website: glitchcharity.co.uk

He For She

A global initiative that seeks to involve men and boys in achieving equality by taking action against harmful gender stereotypes and behaviours.

Website: heforshe.org/en

Hollaback

Offers free virtual, interactive harassment prevention and bystander intervention training.

Website: ihollaback.org

Our Streets Now

Works to inform and campaign against public sexual harassment of women.

Website: ourstreetsnow.org

Muslim Women's Network Helpline

A national specialist faith and culturally sensitive service that supports Muslim women dealing with domestic abuse, honour-based abuse, forced marriage, sexual abuse, sexual harassment, mental health problems and other issues.

Website: mwnhelpline.co.uk
Helpline: 0800 999 5786

National Stalking Helpline

Run by the Suzy Lamplugh Trust, the National Stalking Helpline gives advice and support to victims of stalking.

Website: suzylamplugh.org
Helpline: 0808 802 0300

NHS

The National Health Service has specialist resources aimed at dealing with all forms of violence, and related trauma, experienced by women.

Website: www.nhs.uk
Call: 111

NSPCC FGM Support

The NSPCC provides advice and support on FGM for those at risk and those concerned about others.

Website: www.nspcc.org.uk/what-is-child-abuse/types-of-abuse/female-genital-mutilation-fgm/
FGM Helpline: 0800 028 3550

Paladin Service

A trauma-informed service that works to assist victims of stalking in England and Wales.

Website: paladinservice.co.uk
Call: 0203 866 4107

Rape Crisis

Rape Crisis has centres across England and Wales and online resources for those who have experienced sexual abuse, rape, and all forms of sexual violence.

Website: rapecrisis.org.uk
National telephone helpline: 0808 802 9999

Refuge

National charity providing support for people experiencing domestic violence. Includes specific resources for disabled women.

Website: refuge.org.uk
24-hour domestic violence helpline: 0808 2000 247

Rights of Women

Provides advice and information about the law to women about their legal rights.

Website: rightsofwomen.org.uk
Call: 0207 251 8887
NGT Lite App: 18001 020 7251 6575

Sistah Space

London-based charity working with women and girls of African and Caribbean heritage who have experienced domestic or sexual abuse, or who have lost a loved one to domestic violence.

Website: sistahspace.org
Call: 0207 846 8350

Southall Black Sisters

A group of black and minority women working for women's human rights in the UK.

Website: southallblacksisters.org.uk
Call: 0208 571 9595

Stonewall

A national charity fighting for the rights of LGBT+ people.

Website: stonewall.org.uk
Call: 0800 050 2020

Support After Murder and Manslaughter

Provides peer support services to people bereaved after murder and manslaughter.

Website: samm.org.uk
Helpline: 0121 472 2912
Text: 07342 888570

Surviving Economic Abuse

A charity raising awareness of economic abuse providing support to victims.

Website: survivingeconomicabuse.org

The Survivors Trust

An umbrella agency for specialist rape and sexual abuse services in the UK.

Website: thesurvivorstrust.org
Confidential helpline: 08088 010 818

Women's Aid

A grassroots organisation that provides life-saving services to victims of domestic abuse and works to build a future where domestic abuse is not tolerated.

Website: womensaid.org.uk

Women In Prison

A national charity that supports women affected by the criminal justice system in prison, in the community and through its Women's Centres.

Website: womeninprison.org.uk
Call: 0207 359 667

Acknowledgements

I owe enormous thanks to those who so freely and kindly gave their help, expertise and advice as I was writing this book. The incredible Ngozi Fulani, of Sistah Space, spoke to me for free for nearly an hour to help me better understand the difficulties faced by the women she works with. I have tried my best to reflect her passion, eloquence and acuity in this book.

Many wonderful colleagues offered their help with a generosity that is one of the noblest characteristics of the bar. Bar and feminist legend Helena Kennedy KC was characteristically straightforward and generous in her advice about this book. Sarah Vine KC, Liam Walker KC and Caoilfhionn Gallagher KC have provided concentrated drops of pure wisdom for which I will likely never be able to repay them. Zimran Samuel MBE, a leading expert on FGM, liberally gave his time to discuss it with me on a Saturday while simultaneously juggling small children. And Lucy Reed, who I know only through

Twitter, answered what was certainly a stupid question I had about family law in a matter of minutes, no questions asked.

Thanks are owed to my critical friends: Alex Preston, Alan Simpson and Paul Whittingham, for freely and swiftly providing thoughtful and honest feedback with their usual affectionate mockery.

To Jonathan Drennan, whose motivational emails I appreciated almost as much as his sympathetic voice notes, but nowhere near as much as his stirring Writing Playlists.

To my sister-from-another-mister, Marie-Claire Amuah – a stunning writer and the best co-pupil a woman could ask for – for doing this first, and helping me up.

To the bumblebees, who treat news of promotions and book deals with the same joy that they treat news of marriage and pregnancies.

To Daisy Buchanan for offering unequivocal and kind support from the moment I started writing this (and before), and for being so kind as to share her agent with me.

To Josie Fathers for her excellent and thorough research into Part One, without which I suspect this book would not have been finished for many years.

To the Doughty Street Women for their unremitting sisterhood. I am proud to be one of you.

To the London Writer's Salon for the Writer's Hour,

and to Gladstone's Library, both of which have given me the space to actually write.

To Holly Kyte: a brilliant, speedy and understanding copyeditor.

To Diana Beaumont for being a truly wonderful agent/ literary big sister. I am so glad I met you.

To Jo Thompson at Harper Collins for emailing me one day out of the blue to ask if I'd like to do that thing I'd always wanted to do, and for supporting me unconditionally at every stage since then.

To my wonderful family: to Oliver, to Tom, and to our Grace. To my Dad, for letting me shamelessly steal one of his favourite sayings ('the culture you get is the behaviour you tolerate' – never has it been deployed so mercilessly) and for never expecting any less from his daughters than he did from his son. To my Mum, who does whatever the f*ck she wants, and is still encouraging me to do the same. And to Steve, for everything.